A RECRUIT
ASKS SOME QUESTIONS

A Monograph in

THE POLICE SCIENCE SERIES

Edited by

V. A. LEONARD, *Chairman*

Department, Police Science and Administration
The State College of Washington
Pullman, Washington

A RECRUIT
ASKS SOME QUESTIONS

By

JOHN P. PEPER

Supervisor, Peace Officers Training
California State Department of Education
Bureau of Industrial Education
Sacramento, California

CHARLES C THOMAS · PUBLISHER
Springfield · Illinois · U.S.A.

CHARLES C THOMAS • PUBLISHER
BANNERSTONE HOUSE
301-327 East Lawrence Avenue, Springfield, Illinois, U.S.A.

Published simultaneously in the British Commonwealth of Nations by
BLACKWELL SCIENTIFIC PUBLICATIONS, LTD., OXFORD, ENGLAND

Published simultaneously in Canada by
THE RYERSON PRESS, TORONTO

Library of Congress Catalog Card Number 54–6572

Printed in the United States of America

To my wife
INEZ MACGILLIVRAY PEPER
and daughters
JUANITA, PATRICIA, INEZ CHRISTYE,
and PAULA JAN PEPER

INTRODUCTION

A Recruit Asks Some Questions answers the questions most frequently asked by young men entering police service for the first time. Mr. Peper has brought together between the covers of one book in highly readable form priceless information for the new recruit as he dons a police uniform. "When should I make an arrest?" "How do I investigate a crime?" "Why do I write reports?" "How do I write them?" "How do I interrogate a suspect?" "What are the keys to my advancement in the police profession?" "Can I study to improve my personal efficiency?" "What shall I study?" "How shall I study?"

These and countless other questions are presented and answered by the author, and both questions and answers stem from fifteen years firing line experience as a police officer in one of the nation's top-ranking police departments. Looking back to the day when the Editor put on a police uniform for the first time, A RECRUIT ASKS SOME QUESTIONS would have answered questions whose answers had to come from the rough school of experience. Here is a book that will in all probability become required reading for the American police recruit in every jurisdiction.

In addition, *A Recruit Asks Some Questions* makes available to the profession for the first time a Study Guide which includes tested training materials and procedure for the recruit, as well as for older officers, training supervisors and command personnel. The Study Guide alone, earns for this book a permanent place in the personal library of every American police officer. Furthermore, the methodology of the author in this tool for orientation to the job will prove of interest to workers in the general field of personnel administration everywhere.

V. A. LEONARD
Editor

PREFACE

It is the purpose of this book to analyze several of the questions most frequently asked by new personnel in a police department. All too frequently the administrative and supervisory staffs take for granted the new man or woman in police work is going to like it and if he or she does not, it is the fault of the individual. Instead, they should recognize that they have a tremendous responsibility in properly orientating the recruit, as well as providing guidance for the older officers who desire promotion or need encouragement to maintain their interest.

This book is written with an aim to provide a study guide for the new and perhaps the more experienced officers.

No attempt is made to answer every important question that officers have put to the author during the course of operating several hundred classes in Police Training in California, but those that have been asked most frequently are covered.

While written principally for the officer on the beat, this book will be found helpful to all serious supervisors of police personnel.

The author wishes to express his sincere appreciation to the California State Department of Education, Bureau of Industrial Education, for their permission to reproduce herein as an appendix the *Study Manual and Bibliography for Peace Officers* and to Professor Frank M. Boolsen for his assistance in its preparation.

J. P. P.

CONTENTS

INTRODUCTION vii

PREFACE ix

WHY DID I JOIN THE FORCE? 3

WHAT AM I SUPPOSED TO DO? 5

WHAT IS A GOOD POLICE DEPARTMENT? 8

    WHAT IS A GOOD POLICEMAN? 8

WHY MUST I GO TO SCHOOL? 13

WHY SHOULD A POLICEMAN HAVE TO STUDY? 15

WHAT SHALL I READ? 16

WHAT ELSE SHOULD I READ? 20

SHOULD I STUDY TYPING AND SHORTHAND? 25

WHERE CAN I OBTAIN A STUDY GUIDE? 26

WHY ALL THIS TALK ABOUT PERSONAL CONDUCT,
DISCIPLINE AND MORALE? 27

HOW ABOUT THESE NEWSPAPER REPORTERS? 34

WHAT'S THE USE OF POLICE RECORDS?
HOW DO I USE THEM? 39

HOW DO I CONDUCT MY INVESTIGATIONS AND
HOW DO I WRITE MY REPORTS? 45

RECORD FORMS AND PROCEDURE 52

MAKE USE OF THE RECORDS DIVISION 64

A FINAL WORD OF ENCOURAGEMENT 67

APPENDIX 69

  A Study Manual and Bibliography for Peace Officers 69

    Introduction 71

    Classroom Notetaking 73

    Use of Books by Peace Officers 83

    Use of the Library 97

    Bibliography 117

A RECRUIT
ASKS SOME QUESTIONS

THE RECRUIT ASKS SOME QUESTIONS

WHY DID I JOIN THE FORCE?

As an investigator you will find in all that anyone can say here or elsewhere no advice so valuable as that of Hans Gross in his *Criminal Investigation:* "However inexperienced he will commit no grave mistake if he always remembers the old and precious maxim of the jurist:

> *'Who, what, where, with what, why, how, when? . . .*
> *What was the crime, who did it, when was it done and where,*
> *How done, and with what motive, who in the deed did share?'* "

With a somewhat digressive application it is nevertheless important for the personal benefit of the recruit to emphasize at this time the *Why*—"Why am I becoming a policeman?" You are changing the whole course of your life, so, unless the entrance examinations are a failure, you should have intelligence enough to know why you are here. There are those few of you who have that peculiar enthusiasm for police work for which you are willing to sacrifice the income, security and comfort of other lines of effort in order to gratify that urge for community service and close and frequent human contact; or the thrill of the hunt intrigues you; or the game of matching your wits against those of the law-violator fascinates you. In other words, you are one of those "police-nuts" who throws himself, body and soul, unthinking of time, energy and income, into a life the greatest reward of which—if you live out your years—is the public appraisal: "He is a great detective," or "He is a leading traffic expert," or "He is a brilliant identification man," or "He is a noted criminologist," or "He is one of the country's foremost police administrators."

To many of you the answer is simple: "It is a job until I find something better." Therein is the seed of your early downfall. Of those who have been recruited into the modern American police departments within the past 10 years or so, that is probably

3

the answer of two-thirds. We have not yet reached that point of professionalism in this country that long existed in such countries as Italy, Germany and Austria, where becoming a doctor or a lawyer was prerequisite to entry into the police service. Meanwhile, with standards in our country still below the professional level and pay too low to attract capable men who are seeking lucrative permanent employment, the better American police departments must still rely for the greater number of their recruits upon those young men who look upon the work as a stop-gap in a period of business depression.

You may as well be frank about it. You are welcome just the same; and it is by you that anything in the nature of advice is most needed, because the "police-nut"—the one who, we say, has "police instinct"—will get along pretty well without it, or rather he will make it a point to seek out everything that will make him more proficient in his chosen work. He will solicit recital of lessons of his superiors who have preceded him in the field of trial and error; he will deeply imbed in his brain the mottoes learned from his own successes and failures; he will study every scrap of material available* containing the experiences of others who have walked the beat, broken the alibi of the hardened criminal, used the police scientific laboratory or administered the affairs of a complex organization so difficult as the modern police department.

Whether you expect to stay on permanently or not, many of you will eventually acquire that liking for the work which will make any other kind of activity unattractive. It may take two or three years for you to come to that realization. Others of you will find that prosperity is a long time in turning that promised corner so that you will have spent four or five years in gaining police experience which you will hesitate to throw over in attempting to break into another profession. You will decide to stay and make the most of it. Meanwhile, you may have drifted along in the department, doing just enough to get by and hold your job, while those who entered at the same time, with a better attitude, are just that many years advanced beyond you in the

---

* See Bibliography—Appendix, Part IV.

line of promotion. So, whatever your ultimate intent may be at the time of entry, as an insurance of your own welfare, tackle your job at the outset as if you were wedded to it for life and work and study just as hard as the man who does so through natural interest and aptitude. To those of you who will leave the department, remember that men who have engaged in many occupations in the course of a lifetime assure us that everything which they learned on one job sooner or later and in one way or another was found applicable to all.

From a more unselfish point of view, let us assume that whether you stay a week, month, year or lifetime, just plain common decency and loyalty to the community to whom you have taken your oath to serve, demands that at all times you give the very best that is in you.

WHAT AM I SUPPOSED TO DO?

No one can work intelligently unless he understands the purposes of the organization of which he may be ever so small a member. Fundamentally, there are just two purposes of any police organization: protection of life and protection of property. You may be told that it is preservation of the peace, the arrest and prosecution of violaters of the law, the supervision and control of traffic, the prevention of crime, the aiding of persons in distress of miscellaneous sorts. But you preserve the peace by breaking up the scenes of disorder for what purpose? So that good citizens may go about in the safe enjoyment of their lives and property. You arrest and endeavor to convict the law-violator because he has committed some act which violated a statute designed to protect life or property. You supervise traffic in order to prevent the killing and injuring of people and the damaging of their property; to reduce the social and economic losses entailed by congestion and the retarded traffic stream. You aid in enforcing the health and building regulations because they are designed to eliminate the hazards to healthful living and the free enjoyment of property rights. Even the laws with respect to gambling and other vices are based upon the theory that it is necessary for society to use its corporate facilities to protect the individual who is incapable of resisting temptation leading to the detriment of his own healthful living and enjoyment of property or the welfare and the lives of those who are dependent upon him and his property for support. By enforcement of these laws, the apprehension of the violator and his punishment by fine or confinement, it is further the theory that the punishment discourages that particular offender from again breaking society's rules, that it sets an example for others who will thus be deterred from engaging in the same unlawful practices; and, certainly, while an offender is incarcerated, whether he is reformed or not, during the time of his confinement he is not molesting the lives or the property of others. So it is well to keep at least in the back of your mind throughout your career that the purposes of yourself and your organization, whatever the particular activity in which you may be engaged, are fundamentally and ultimately the protection of life and property.

As already indicated, to enable you to protect life and property, the legislative authorities of your city and county, state, and federal governments, have passed laws and made it your duty to enforce them. This has saved you the necessity of determining in your own mind, up to a certain point, what acts constitute attacks upon the welfare of lives or property rights; or, rather, what the legislative authorities have decided in that respect.

This makes necessary at this point some discussion as to the officer's interpretation of the spirit of the law. It is not so simple as learning all of the laws and then going out and arresting everyone found violating them. You would never get six blocks away from your station in any day's tour of duty. The law, for instance, states that if you drive an automobile at a speed greater than twenty miles an hour in certain designated localities you have violated the law; and yet you would be only making an ass of yourself by bringing into court everyone who traveled twenty-one miles an hour in a twenty-mile zone. How about twenty-five miles? Probably in ninety per cent of these cases you would still not concern yourself. How about thirty miles? Finer discretion is needed as much depends upon the density of traffic, the number of pedestrians, whether night or day, whether the street is obstructed, wet or dry, paved or unpaved, etc. The law requires that on streets appropriately signed a full stop must be made before entering the street on which the signs are posted. The law says nothing about slowing down—it says "Stop." It says nothing about the officer using his judgment, contingent upon the volume of traffic in the near vicinity of the intersection which the motorist is about to enter; yet to arrest a man who has slowed almost to a stop and, carefully noting the absence of traffic in either direction, proceeded without endangering anyone, would stamp the officer as an arbitrary fool. Obviously, the officer is required to exercise judgment, even in the enforcement of certain laws which plainly give the officer the right, if not the duty, to make an arrest.

At what point does he have the duty as well as the right? When should he make an arrest and when—although the law does not give the officer the specific authority, and kindness and tact must be exercised when employing such an alternative— should he excuse, caution, or reprimand?

In crimes of violence such as murder, assault and rape, or in crimes for gain such as larceny, burglary, robbery, forgery, and gross cheat, clearly common sense as well as the law allows you no discretion. They and many others are crimes of moral turpitude, the wrongfulness of which is definitely known to the perpetrator. They are usually premeditated. They involve distinct moral, as well as legal guilt. Consequently, such offenders must, without exception, be taken before the bar of justice to pay any penalty which the law may inflict.

But in countless instances in the enforcement, particularly of traffic and other regulatory ordinances, the officer must assume the function of the prosecutor, judge, and jury, as well as, or rather than, merely the arresting officer. There is a great field of police duty necessitating the exercise of such discrimination. Moreover, perhaps an average of two-thirds of the patrolman's daily tour of duty is taken up with matters requiring this kind of judgment in adjusting the difficulties of citizens without arrest and in solving their problems where no matter of law is involved. Do not think that merely memorizing the statutes is going to guide you in more than the minor portion of the volume of your official work.

However, there is a borderland of offenses, including a large number which may or may not be merely technical, where the intelligent and conscientious officer is bothered in his own mind as to whether an arrest should be made. The safest policy in such instances is to arrest, assuming that the officer can be sure that the violation, at least technically, has been committed, and arrest is therefore authorized, taking into account, of course, the laws of arrest with respect to offenses not committed in the officer's presence, as well as the advisability of delay pending completion of the investigation. When such an honest doubt does exist, particularly where the offender's identity might be lost in delay, it is safest to err on the side of arrest.

After all, the officer can always take this attitude: "I did not make the law. It is not my duty to reason whether the law is right or wrong but to decide whether the law has been violated; if so, it is my further duty to arrest and present the case for determination by the court."

In this connection, remember that the law is no respector of persons. Each case should be decided upon its merit, as such, and not upon the elements of the defendant's friendship, political influence, or financial or social standing in the community; excepting the few instances where some degree of immunity, dependent upon official position, is recognized by law.

To a large extent you must rely upon the instruction of your superiors, the advice of those longer in the game—not only of those in your own department but of those others whose experiences with police and related social problems have been published—and, out of all that, combined with your own experience, you must increase your own store of social intelligence so that in the enforcement of your official duties and in the application of your skilled police technique, you will exhibit the thing inadequately termed "common sense," which, it has been truthfully said, is so very uncommon.

WHAT IS A GOOD POLICE DEPARTMENT?
WHAT IS A GOOD POLICEMAN?

Every ambitious officer is rightfully interested in his own advancement. So far as it is humanly possible to judge, advancement should be the reward of superiority in performance of duty.

The man who demonstrates his ability to accomplish the most results is the man who should head the promotion list. What is the measure of performance for an individual officer? Whatever the answer may be it should equally suffice for the question, "What is the measure of performance for the entire department?" Just as in the case of the department, so in the case of the individual officer, it is difficult to compare the performance of one with the other. But the "four-flusher" should be warned forthwith. Again quoting from Hans Gross, " 'Obtaining a result' must not be confused with 'producing an effect.' " Every police administrator has encountered the "personality boy," who can give an intelligent outline of the task to be accomplished, make glowing promises of early success and produce nothing more than a fine, grammatically perfect and exhaustive record of a lot of things that have been done—excepting the one thing in which the administrator or anyone is most interested—and that is the successful termination of the job.

Getting back to the fundamental police purposes, protection of life and property, how can the officer's work be recorded so as to measure his success in these two respects? Just as the work of the whole department can be recorded to measure the same results—by recording the number of cases reported and assigned and the number of such cases cleared and noting the relation of cases known with cases *cleared.* Not how many cases but what percentage of those known cases were cleared. Assuming that the department is intelligently administered, beat studies are made so as to provide that the work-load on each beat is, as nearly as possible, equal to that on each other beat. We are not forgetting, of course, that conditions on some beats require the constant attention of an officer while, at the same time, there are few reported cases. But, in the large, the work loads on the various beats will be approximately the same and the records of such work will approximate each other in number.

Assuming that on two adjoining beats each officer in the course of a month investigates one hundred cases. One man clears 50 of his cases, the other 75. One has a clearance, therefore, of 50%, whereas the other exceeds him by 25%. The officer with the better record may have been favored with better luck in any one month or for several months, but, in the course of a year or years, the man with the highest percentage of clearances, it is relatively safe to assume, is the most efficient officer. It may also be that one officer, by his more efficient patrol, makes it less possible for criminals to commit offenses so that are only 75 cases reported on his beat, out of which he clears 50, or a percentage of 66 $^2/_3$. So, your work will be judged, first of all, upon your ability to keep your beat "clean," that is, to keep down the number of offenses; and, secondly, upon the percentage of reported cases cleared. Remember, too, that efficiency can be determined in a relative sense, by putting another man on your beat and studying his record in relation to yours by means of the standards just mentioned.

In order that patrolmen, for example, may not think they are deprived of credit when a case is completed by detectives, let it be thoroughly understood that full credit is given to every man who plays a material part in the closing of a case. As a matter of fact, successful cooperation with detectives and other officers is a mark of much greater efficiency and general reliability than if you tried to "hog" your cases to yourself.

There are, of course, certain other factors to be considered, such as keeping out of trouble, your promptness in attendance for daily duty and special assignments, your courtesy in dealing with the public, your cooperation with your fellow officers, your general good conduct as a representative of an organization which must be jealous of its reputation for setting the example for other members of the community to follow in their contacts one with another. It is not enough for you to be efficient in the apprehension of other violators if you yourself endanger your own good name and that of the department by immoral, illegal, or otherwise vicious conduct. The department cannot tolerate among its members an insultor of the public, an habitual drunkard, a liar, a cheat, a double-crosser, a buck-passer, a sex libertine, or one who knowingly and wilfully violates the laws which he is sworn to enforce.

But it is not, by any means, enough merely to have a negatively good record by never being guilty of any of these transgressions. There are men who are shrewd enough just to keep out of trouble—and that is all they do.   They never accomplish any positive acts of the kind for which they are employed, and are therefore useless and should be soon eliminated.

Let it be emphasized—an officer should be judged by the successful termination of his investigations.   Nice appearance, courtesy, unusual physique, keen mentality, initiative, courage, loyalty, and a host of other qualities, mean nothing unless you get results.   Particularly to the recruit should the importance of performance as a measure of worth be emphasized.   You have all been highly selected, as far as it is possible to do short of actual trial over a period of time.   You are superior individuals, considerably above the average, as far as can be judged by known formal tests of physique, character, and general intelligence.   The best that an administrator can do is to assume that one superior in the qualities just mentioned will probably be a more efficient policeman than a man without them or with them to a lesser degree.   It has been proved in long years of experience that the assumption is a safe one to perhaps a 75% extent.   But it is up to you to prove that you are among the 75% rather than among the 25% who fail or who never attain to more than mediocre proficiency.   The proof lies in your performance.

About the most that tests can determine with respect to a candidate for a police position is physical condition and general intelligence.   To some extent character can be ascertained by studying his previous employment record, recommendations of personal references and previous conduct in general.   Among new men who have not been extensively tried in work as gruelling as that of the police, personal references do not mean much and character qualities must also be determined by trial under the exigencies of police work.

We may list five indispensable basic qualities of character outstanding above, or rather, including all others in the good policeman, rated in order of importance as follows: Loyalty, courage, interest, energy, general intelligence.   The determination of these qualities comes in exactly the reverse order.

When the recruit comes into the department about all that can be said with certainty is with respect to his intelligence.   To a much lesser extent, something is known, through the tests, of his energy and interest in police work, although it may be that the energy and interest demonstrated in the tests is mainly an energetic interest in getting a job—any kind of a job. During the first few days and weeks of his employment the administrators get more convincing evidence of the recruit's energy. In the following weeks and months it is discovered whether the expenditure of that energy is because of interest in the job or merely holding a job. Sometimes, by fortuitous circumstance, within the first few days of a recruit's experience he will encounter dangerous physical and moral obstacles that will indicate to his superiors whether he "can take it," or be forced to relinquish his position to a man of sterner stuff.

Loyalty, the most valuable quality of all, frequently requires years in the testing. A man may, through his intelligence, energy, interest and courage, be eminently successful and even reach a position of command; then, after trusted years of service, in just one crisis, wipe out all the good that he has accomplished by a single act of disloyalty.

Now, don't get the wrong conception of what constitutes loyalty. Loyalty does not require an honest man to carry out orders which are grossly illegal or immoral. Nor does it require that an honest man overlook or protect his employer or fellow employee in corrupt practice. Loyalty is a general philosophical term, the meaning of which we must determine for ourselves. But it is certain that loyalty to an ideal may transcend loyalty to an individual. We are correct in having many loyalties at the same time, none conflicting with another. But frequently one loyalty must give way before the other and loyalty to an ideal of service, let us say, compels us to take a stand which is tragically interpreted by many honest persons as disloyalty to an individual. Decision, in such conflict of loyalties, to follow the greater loyalty to the exclusion of the lesser, brings into play the quality of courage which is always present in the display of the highest loyalty. The occasional difficulty of following the ideal of loyalty only emphasizes its superlative value.

Every police organization has a number of old "work-horses," whose early educational opportunities were poor, who plug along through the years with nothing but loyalty, enthusiasm for the job and energy which is exerted with bulldog courage and tenacity. While they never do anything spectacular, they continue to bring in the crooks and clear up their cases. While they do not scintillate with flashes of brilliance, they are steady, methodical producers; and, while nothing great is expected of them, the chief can be absolutely certain of a steady, ordinary, good output. Though he knows they will never reach the heights, he is just as certain they will never sink to the depths of disloyalty.

As August Vollmer once said, "Give me one hard-working dumb-bell in preference to a whole platoon of scintillating nitwits."

WHY MUST I GO TO SCHOOL?

You may confidently expect that for at least the first few years of your service as a police officer you will be subjected to compulsory classes of instruction—unfortunately, and unjustly from one point of view, on your own time. If the American policeman is to be something more than the old type gun-toter and club-wielder, he must be trained. There are a few American police departments, such as New York and Los Angeles, large enough and with recruits coming into the department in sufficiently large numbers at one time to justify a police training school of weeks or months at the expense of the city before the recruit is put out on a beat. This is not possible in the smaller departments. The only way in which such schools can be conducted for the smaller departments is by centralized state or sectional schools to which a number of such smaller departments may send their recruits* or graduation from which the department may require as a qualification for employment. Although there is a nation-wide movement under way to establish educational facilities of this type, it will be years before they adequately provide for all the needs. In most departments, it would be prohibitive in cost to maintain a training school staff for dribbling groups of two or three recruits. A larger number, including those who have been in the department for some time, must make up the class and obviously

* California Program for Peace Officers Training, California State Department of Education.

some of them, if not all of them, must attend on their own time. This is one of the objectionable features of municipal police service at the present time, which the recruit must accept with good grace and be grateful for the opportunity given him to increase his own efficiency.

Don't ever get the idea that you are clever enough to be a policeman without training and study. Perhaps the most common among the felony crimes is burglary, yet probably there has never been a recruit to any department who, in spite of his previous study, was able to give an accurate and complete definition of the elements of that crime. As a matter of fact, just recently a Chief of Police conducted a short surprise quiz on his men. Not one of the 23 were able to correctly define burglary, which constitutes our greatest major crime problem.

In the local press not long ago, one writer who enjoys considerable popularity, criticizing the department's educational policies, made the statement that police work is nothing much anywhere but "a gun and a club." By making such a statement he demonstrated either abysmal ignorance or despicable demagoguery. If ignorance, it is in spite of the readily ascertainable information that the rightfully vaunted superiority of the European police is based upon a selective and educational system which in some places requires their officers to hold doctors' degrees and show other evidence of professional capacity and training. This particular journalist, if he were jealous enough of his own reliability as a *journalist,* should be ready to answer the challenge of the Prussian system, for example, where policemen were trained for seven years before being assigned to actual work on their own individual responsibility. The Parisian police, justly famous in fact and fiction, have been found inadequately trained to cope with the increasing difficulty of modern police problems. Those who hereafter become commissars must be university graduates, while the second class, inspectors, must have an education which is the equivalent of our junior colleges. Just a moment's sober and sincere thought should obviate the necessity of citing the European precedent.

Continuing with our example of burglary, what good is a gun and a club as the sole physical and mental equipment of a police-

man if he doesn't know when the crime of burglary has been committed so as to justify the use of that gun or club in making an
arrest? Few important criminals are apprehended at the scene
of their crimes. Then what mysterious power does the gun or
club have to point to the identity of the burglar who is not apprehended at the scene of his crime? How, if he doesn't know the
corpus delicti, can the officer recognize, collect and prepare for
court the evidence necessary to convict the burglar? Of what
service is the mere possession of his gun and club in that predica-
ment? The *journalist's* statement, smugly designed to display his
Shavian profundity, is too silly to merit the recognition of comment were it not for the unfortunate fact that his shallow view is
representative of an appreciably large section of the community
from which, in spite of carefully selective processes, some of our
recruits may come.

WHY SHOULD A POLICEMAN HAVE TO STUDY?

Don't stop at gracefully tolerating mandatory instruction. You
have in your own police library as good a collection of publications relating to police work as will be found in any department.
Additions are continually being made. Yet they are useless unless *used*. Here again you will hear the addle-pated objection,
"You can learn police work only by experience; what we need is
the good practical man."

Suppose the same attitude were taken toward other profes-
sions? Suppose we said to the thousands of students spending
eight to 15 years of their lives in the university lecture room,
library, laboratory and clinic, "Don't waste your time with such
theoretical stuff—get yourself a kit of doctor's tools and go out
and learn by experience." As a matter of fact, that was literally
done in former years and is still practiced in uncivilized portions
of the globe. But in more advanced localities people soon re-
fused to trust their lives to the untrained hands and minds of the
jolly old "practical" saw-bones and demanded professionally
trained physicians and surgeons. True, to attain perfection in
any profession requires, in addition to the years of schooling,
practical experience in the field. How do you suppose an advance

in medical science is almost simultaneously adopted by leading physicians the world over? Is it possible that each doctor, working entirely within his own limited practice, discovers improved techniques by himself at exactly the same time as the others? Of course not. It is by the student method of reading the publications of one another and their professional journals, in which they exchange their experiences. Otherwise it is possible, let us say, that in the city of Vienna physicians by word of mouth and their own individual experiences might have attained some degree of their present day proficiency without the reading or the publication of a single book or professional journal, and that this "practical" policy were maintained in all the other cities of the world. In the city of New York, it is conceivable that we still would be treated by Indian witch doctors.

It is true, we do learn *solely* by experience, but most of it is through the experiences of others recorded in books and periodicals as well as by personal instruction through the advice and demonstration of our superiors, our fellow workers, the university and convention lecturer, and the clinic or seminar director. We are still suffering along with the "practical" policeman, who learns his precious little through his own limited experience, and paying for it with our lives and yearly losses of *billions* of dollars of private and public wealth. Slowly, however, the analogy is seeping through our lumbering minds, and the continental attitude toward the training of policemen is gradually developing.

You can't do all your reading in one year any more than you can obtain all the necessary personal experience within that length of time. You can never stop studying if you are to progress, any more than you can ever reach the time when you will cease to profit by the instruction of your superiors, the advice of your fellows and your own experience.

Leaders in the police field consider that in spite of long lives solely devoted to furthering of police work as a science, they are still barely on the threshold of their objective.

WHAT SHALL I READ?

Here is a suggested reading course—a practical one if you will—which should be completed in the order given within the first year of your service.

Rules and Regulations, including its appendixes. You should have thoroughly absorbed its contents within the first week. In one department recently one of the new officers, at the time of this writing, has forfeited his weekly days off for several months for an infraction of the rules which would have been avoided had he studied his rules and regulations. In the absence of any other instruction, it contains a fair outline of the objectives and policies of the department and the duties and responsibilities of its individual members.

General Orders. Read them from the very beginning, up to and including the very latest and be sure that you familiarize yourself with each new order as it comes out. They should not only be read but studied carefully, noting where one general order modifies or supersedes one or more which preceded it.

The Policeman, by Cornelius Cahalane. This is a small book of which there are several copies in the public library of your city. It is a book which should satisfy the demand for the practical. It is written by an officer long in the service of the New York police department, one of this country's greatest metropolitan organizations. With the exception of the chapter on horses, which has no bearing upon your local police duties at the present time, and the chapter on records which is worse than useless—except as an illustration of most departments' backwardness in record procedure—every chapter is sound and the advice which it contains is applicable in the city of Berkeley, in the city of Los Angeles or in Podunk Center, just as it is in the city of New York or in any other community in the world. It is not the best book that could be written on the subject, but it is easily understandable, compact, and deals with the problems which the new patrolman will immediately encounter. This, too, should easily be read and its lessons fairly well absorbed within the first week of your service.

Municipal Ordinances. This body of law, more probably than any other, must be read and memorized or you can have no conception of what you are to enforce. Many of the ordinances—in fact most of them—are regulatory. They involve no moral principle, the violation of which you recognize from your common conception of right and wrong. August Vollmer relates that he once asked the Chief of Police of a large American department to explain his methods of instructing recruits. This somewhat notorious "practical" exponent of the police art replied, "I don't give them no training. I call them into my office and say, 'You guys know the Ten Commandments, don't you? Well, go out and arrest every so-and-so violating them.'" Now it is submitted that the recruit has enough difficulty depending on his own resources without further hastening his mental breakdown by trying to make the Ten Commandments fit the problems which city ordinances are designed to solve. All of which serves to say, "save yourself a lot of trouble and learn your city ordinances."

Penal or Criminal Code of your State. Study particularly those laws covering arrest procedure and those defining the crimes which the patrolman is daily required to recognize and investigate, such as those dealing with juveniles and those offending against them, common nuisances, drunkenness, assaults, sex offenses, larceny, gross cheat, forgery, burglary, robbery and homicide. It is important not merely to have a general idea of these crimes, but it is necessary to memorize the statutory definitions of them because every element in the definition is of vital importance in order to enable you to obtain convictions. Many cases are lost because the officer has failed to acquire evidence with respect to one of the several elements in the corpus delicti and the reason why he has so failed is because he neglected to inform himself as to what each of them is and the importance attached to it. In spite of the layman's belief, legislators do not make laws more or less lengthy merely to demonstrate their knowledge of the English language in general and legal terminology in particular. Every word counts. If you don't take this advice, you will learn to your sorrow later, when you discover the reason for your failure to obtain a conviction in an important case, that it does.

Policemen are prone to criticize the prosecutor or the judge or the jury when their cases are thrown out of court or the defendants are acquitted. All of these other forces of criminal justice sometimes err because the machinery is operated by men not much different than yourself. But probably in nine out of ten such failures the fault will be your own because you don't know what you are paid to know. You have taken the advice of the opinionated journalist who told us that police work means only a gun and a club, or you have taken the advice of some other officer who has told you that to study is a lot of bunk, that it is not "practical", and that what you should do is go out and learn from experience. The one who gives you such advice is, without exception, still at the bottom of the ladder and his "experience" hasn't enabled him to eliminate the mistakes which he makes today just as he did last month, last year or fifteen years ago.

What the Policeman Should Know, by James J. Skehan, is a book similar to Cahalane's, The Policeman, and as good or better.

Criminal Investigation, Hans Gross. If you did no more studying in your whole career—not merely reading—beyond that already listed and including this great work almost reverently termed by the old-timers, "The Policeman's Bible," you would be better prepared for your job as a policeman than two-thirds of those of almost any department. Hans Gross was a great scientist, doctor of laws, magistrate, criminal investigator, psychologist and university professor for more than half a century and became outstanding in his native land, which ranks so high in all that relates to police efficiency, Austria. There has never been, and it is doubtful if there ever will be, a man so capable in so many divisions of the machinery of justice. To those who might observe that the book was translated from the German in 1911 and subsequent editions have been English revisions, and who therefore think that it is too old to be of service, let it be said that *Criminal Investigation* is not only the first book of its kind but the only book of its kind and that the technique of investigation and much of the scientific material will be as valuable a thousand years from now as it was when Hans Gross first set it down as a collection of his rich life-time *experience*. Those who want the thoroughly *practical* and who want to learn by real experience need search no further. It is only because of its exhausting volume that it has not been set down at the head of this list, for to thoroughly absorb its contents requires not only one reading but several, which should be spread over a period of a year, and in subsequent years it is well to frequently go back and refresh your memory of its contents. Some small portions of it are obsolete or they contain information peculiarly valuable in Europe, but even among these otherwise obsolete and territorially-limited portions there is much profitable analogy with the modern crime situation that can be drawn. So read it all carefully at least once and in your subsequent readings concentrate on the selected bulk of it, which is universal in its application.

WHAT ELSE SHOULD I READ?

It is assumed that you, the modern recruit, have an educational background which includes a fair layman's knowledge of psychology, history, and the technique and purposes of social organizations in general. But if you are not going to continue as a layman all your life, if you are going to acquire the more thorough background which you will need if you are to become a professional in the police service, you must continue to read in various fields. For instance, if you aspire to become an intelligent police administrator you should study, in an organized fashion, administrative theory not only governing your own department and those preceding and contemporary with it, but you should study the history, theory and present set-up of other governmental agencies, legislative, judicial and administrative, for every one of them has some bearing, more or less direct, upon your own organization and ultimately upon your own individual job. Crime is not merely a police problem, it is a community problem, and unless you know something of the responsibility which each official unit assumes as its own or should assume as its own, or what their relation as individual groups and as a combination have with your own, you are going to die without making to the cause of good government the contribution of which you are capable.

In outlining your reading schedule, split it up into several main fields such as those studies dealing with the human mind—psychology and psychiatry; administration; patrol procedure; traffic regulation; laboratory methods of identification; questioned documents; criminology; etc.

Let us assume, for example, that you begin with *psychology* and psychiatry to enable you better to know how and why so-called normal and abnormal human individuals and groups behave as they do. Now we hear a lot of scoffing from the "practical" type of person who is always talking in general terms about "common sense" and "just using your head." But if all bodies of knowledge were ignored just because of quackery, none would survive. There is much unsound practice in the medical science, for example. Some of it is willful quackery and much of it has not yet been put upon an adequately proved basis. But no intelligent person would advocate chucking all of it because of imperfection in parts. So it is with psychology. Much of it is incomplete. Much of it is bad. But there is now a large body of proven principles having the definite practical value of aiding us to more intelligently deal with other human beings. The very nature of our work is such that not a single bit is divorced from the human equation.

It is suggested that you start with some popular work in the general field. Karl Menninger's *The Human Mind* is interesting, instructive, and is recommended by many conservative professional psychologists. You should have it in your own library. Dorsey's *Why We Behave Like Human Beings* is not so highly recommended by professionals but they do suggest it as a means of creating popular interest in the subject and an easily acquired basis for more serious study. After reading one of these popular works it is recommended that you read one of the better university texts such as Woodworth's *Psychology,* which is a widely used university textbook in general psychology. *Intelligence, Its Manifestations and Measurements* by Boynton is recommended for those who have the general background and are interested in the applied field. After you have built up a groundwork, read *Criminal Psychology* by Hans Gross, the author of *Criminal Investigation.* This is a difficult work and must be tackled as such. Some of it has been proved inadequate or faulty by subsequent research, but with a modern psychology background you will be able to choose that which is good and reject that which is less accurate and worthwhile. Some of it you will have already read in *Criminal Investigation.*

After your preparation in psychology, to be able to recognize at least those insane and otherwise abnormal persons whose mental conditions bring them in contact with the police, you should study some standard text on psychiatry such as *Rosanoff* or *White,* both of which may be found in your public library.

Now, it is not advisable to read exhaustively on any subject without sandwiching in something from another field of police study. Do not get the impression that it is recommended that you read all of these as a continued, uninterrupted project. They are all mentioned together, just as will be those dealing with the other branches, in order that the references may be grouped according to subject.

In order to understand the policies of the *administration* and more intelligently, and consequently with more pleasure, perform your part in the program you should, early in your career, read some good works on that subject. There are several. Fosdick's two books on European Police and the American Police systems have long been recognized for their worth. Leonard's *Police Organization and Management* is more recent and to my mind more interesting, while equally as instructive. An excellent guide for the student of police administration is the California State Department of Education book, *Police Organization and Administration*, co-authored by August Vollmer, Frank M. Boolsen, and this author. There are some others and many that touch upon the subject in discussing criminology in general.

For *detective* and *patrol procedure*, in addition to those earlier mentioned, there are *Criminal Investigation* by Fricke, the *Police Manual* by Chandler, *One Thousand Police Questions* by Fricke, Luke S. May's *Scientific Murder Investigation* and a number of others.

On *general criminology*, the causes and treatment of crime and criminals, including administrative principles, there are numerous good books in your own library. One of the more recent and interesting is Cantor's *Crime, Criminals and Criminal Justice.* Sutherland's *Principles of Criminology*, a 1934 publication, is especially worthwhile.

Specializing on the subject of *traffic*, there is only one book, of which there are several copies, *Traffic Officers Manual* by Clarence Taylor. Taylor is a practical man with several years experience as a patrolman and traffic expert in the Berkeley Police Department, graduate engineer in the University of California, two years as an Erskine fellowship student in traffic engineering at Harvard University, and for some time past the state traffic engineer for Massachusetts. He is generally considered to be the world's leading traffic expert.

To supplement the information contained in the general works and, more especially, in Gross's books—if you are interested, as you should be, in more recent developments in the physically *scientific field* of criminology and desire to be better informed in the way in which experts may assist you—read *Forensic Chemistry and Scientific Criminal Investigation* by Lucas; Wolfe's *Forgotten Clues; Recent Advances in Forensic Medicine* by Smith and Glaister; *The Scientific Detective and Expert Witness,* and in addition to these there are several other volumes on forensic medicine which you will do well to consult as references in any point of law having a medical aspect.

While you are still in the Patrol Division you are likely to be assigned to some case requiring expert knowledge in the examination of *questioned writings* such as forgery or threatening and extortion letters. Especially if you like that kind of work, it is well that you study to become an expert examiner of questioned documents. At the present time there are few officers who can qualify for that rating and there is one chance that is absolutely certain; but it, like so many higher positions in the department, requires hard preparation. You won't get your experience by merely wishing or doing your studying by reading "true" love romances or even by confining yourself to the magazines featuring true detective stories, written for popular entertainment rather than for practical instruction. You will have to begin by studying such works as Osborne's two books, *Questioned Documents* and the *Problem of Proof.* Osborne, incidentally, is the recognized world's leading expert. *Classification and Identification of Handwriting,* by Lee and Abbey, is good, particularly for simplicity of method. Both, particularly Lee, are long-experienced police officers as well as specialists in this field.

Records of one department show that of the 12,516 persons arrested by this department during the year ending December 31st, 3897 of them were under the age of eighteen. These figures, without further comment, indicate the tragic importance of doing all that the police department can do by itself or in cooperation with other social agencies to prevent juveniles from becoming

criminals or for quick and effective curative treatment after their
first contact with the police. One of the surest ways of keeping
your own beat clean and thereby making for yourself a good
record, is to deal intelligently with the boys and girls living,
working or playing on that beat. Now you may have your own
pre-conceived notions about what classes of children become
criminals and what can be done to prevent them or to cure them,
but until you have read what is said by trained experts, who have
given their lives to the study, you can not claim to be prepared
to handle your part of that problem. You may disagree with them
if you like, even as they disagree to some extent among themselves, but you have no right to do so without knowing what
they have to say in their various publications. *The Individual
Delinquent,* by William Healy, will usefully supplement the
briefer dealing with the problem which you will find in many
other books already mentioned.

The list just given is not exhaustive of the material in your own
library. There are many others, some in the nature of worthwhile
criminal autobiographies such as *Stealing Through Life* by Er-
nest Booth, and *You Can't Win,* by Jack Black.

It is suggested only that the books already mentioned are of
the best in their respective fields and that you should read at
least one in each group as early as you can and follow them up by
reading others as time will allow. You will undoubtedly discover that, after you have done the suggested minimum of reading, you will be inclined to specialize and you are encouraged
to do so. There is need for some specialization. If you wish to
become a ballistics expert, for example, by all means express your
desire to do so.

Every officer in the department should know at least the *classification and uses of fingerprints.* Practically all of the major
burglaries occurring within one city in a whole year were cleared
with nothing more to start with than a single fingerprint. You,
as an officer who will almost certainly have a part in the investigation of a burglary within your first month of service, should know
how and where fingerprints are left at the scene of a crime, how
to discover them and what to do with them after they are found.
You should know the limitations of fingerprints as well as their

positive uses; what they can do as well as what they cannot do. Read *Classification and Uses of Fingerprints* by Sir E. R. Henry and *Fingerprint Instructor* by Kuhne. If you wish to use your spare time to make yourself expert in the classification and identification of fingerprints, the facilities of the records and staff of the Identification Bureau of the Records Division will be made available to you.

It is not enough with respect to *law* merely to know the definition of crimes. It is of vital importance that you know your powers and limitations in making arrests and what constitutes evidence, how it is made available for court and the rules of its admission and how to conduct yourself as a witness—if you do your job, hardly a week will pass without your being called as such. You have in your department library the *Law of Arrest,* Stevens; *Cases on Criminal Law and Procedure,* Mikell; *On the Witness Stand,* Munsterberg; *Principles of Judicial Proof,* Wigmore; standard references of judges and lawyers engaged in criminal law.

SHOULD I STUDY TYPING AND SHORTHAND?

Among the most valuable studies that you can pursue is *typing.* On every case to which you are assigned you will have to type some kind of a report and almost always on your own time after coming off the beat. The more you do on your beat, the more reports you will have to write. It naturally follows then that you will save yourself hundreds of hours within a couple of years if you know how to type rapidly. This ability can best be acquired by attending some public or private commercial school and learning the touch system. Then, too, rapid typing ability enables you to record your thoughts with greater accuracy and completeness so that you will not unintentionally omit important facts.

Moreover, after you have completed a course in the touch system of typing, you will have acquired during the course of it a neater style and a better vocabulary, which will be shown in your reports. A neatly arranged, properly spelled, and accurately typed report always creates a better impression in the minds of superiors who read it than if it is sprawled over the page in an amateurish fashion, with frequent typographical errors—even though it may contain no more information. Accept this from one who has read hundreds of thousands of reports; and keep in mind in this, as in all things, that your work is measured not only by an ideal standard but by comparison with the current contributions of others.

While a working knowledge of *shorthand* is not as essential as expert typing ability, it too will save you incalculable time. It will enable you to note all the facts discovered in your investigation and obtain that which is often so vitally important to the prosecution of a criminal case: verbatim statements of witnesses and suspects. But it means hard work. Assuming you have better than average intelligence, the education you are required to have for membership in the department and an energetic mind with the power to concentrate, 500 hours of earnest effort will make you a fair stenographer.

Remember that from this time on the competition for promotion will become keener. Every facility within the department and every assistance that can be solicited among scientists and scientific laboratories in the community will be placed at your disposal if you show real interest and a promise of ability in your chosen specialty. Remember that there is always some specialty in which every man can excel. It is up to the individual officer to determine what one specialty his shall be and work at it.

Remember, too, that if the department as a whole is ever to receive the higher salaries to which we of the profession believe we are entitled, every man will have to do his part in demonstrating to the public that he and his fellows are worth more money. It may be slow in coming but you are not going to hasten the day by just getting by, sliding along on the hope that it will be handed to you on a silver platter without continuous effort to improve the quality and increase the quantity of your own work.

WHERE CAN I OBTAIN A STUDY GUIDE?

This question has frequently been asked by both recruits and experienced officers. To meet this need the author, with the cooperation of Professor Frank M. Boolsen, prepared a course for use by officers and police instructors. This course was mimeographed and made available to all peace officers by the California Program for Police Training of the California State Department of Education. The California State Department of Education has made this course, *Study Manual and Bibliography for Peace Officers,* available to the author and given permission to include it as an appendix to this text. You should study this manual carefully.

WHY ALL THIS TALK ABOUT PERSONAL CONDUCT, DISCIPLINE AND MORALE?

When a civilian takes oath of office as a policeman and accepts his badge of authority, he is thereby making himself a target for criticism, favorable or unfavorable, by every member of the community. If you don't realize it when you take the oath, you will have the fact borne in upon you as soon as you engage in your official duties. You are in a position comparable with that of the young minister accepting the vestments of his calling. You must remember that in the complexity of modern society, with its criminal laws sooner or later directly affecting every member of the community, the policeman, whose special duty it is to enforce those laws, encounters in every case to which he is assigned not only the active enmity of the offender but frequently of the victim, who from the outset is at least skeptical as to the officer's ability to successfully enact the role of that victim's servant.

The American people in general do not have much confidence in their police officers. It has become almost traditional for a large section of the American public to distrust the motives and disparage the abilities of its law-enforcing officials. This attitude is in part justified by reason of malperformance throughout the long past. But much of the fault is that of this same distrustful public. For work which, if properly done, requires professional ability and the highest character and courage to withstand its physical and moral dangers, it pays its officers as little in some localities as it pays its janitors and in no community is the pay yet adequate. John Smith, "citizen tax-payer," squawks as if he personally were paying all of that inadequate little out of his own pocket. Every month he pays more out in service bills for gas, lights and power than he does for his whole year's portion of the whole police department's salary. Although a dozen men in the office of a single public utility in any community may each be receiving a salary of more than $10,000 a year for doing a little work that many of their under-paid clerks could do just as well, John Smith, "citizen tax-payer" hasn't the intelligence to realize that he pays a much higher portion of those large public utilities salaries of $10,000 a head, than he does of the miserable "flat-foot's" yearly stipend. In the first instance, John Smith takes what he gets at whatever price he is required to pay, without a growl. In the second he expects the miraculous and is satisfied with nothing less than human perfection. Failing to get it, he is ready to damn the policeman, damn the Chief, and damn the whole department to eternal perdition; especially if you should hand him—or his wife—a ticket for failing to make a boulevard stop when he "knows" he did and you know he didn't. You see, the laws which he insists upon his legislators making are good laws in his estimation but they are designed for the other fellow and the other fellow is just another John Smith, "citizen taxpayer." Because of a host of reasons, any one of them sufficient in John Smith's mind, you are labeled as a morally lecherous, blundering dim-wit, and dong-dong-grabber. So while you must gratefully acknowledge the good wishes of perhaps the majority of the citizens, you must be continually vigilant so as to avoid giving that large remainder no opportunity for successfully attacking your own moral character and ability and, as a consequence, the moral character and ability of the entire department.

An officer discharged from a certain department was told, when his personal activities became questionable, that the policy of the department was not to interfere with an officer's private affairs until those affairs endangered the efficiency of the department, and it was pointed out to him that if the allegation of a citizen were true that he, as a member of the department and a married man, was having sexual relations with and engaging in drunken parties with a young ward of the juvenile court, then, quite apart from it being a violation of the criminal law which he was sworn to uphold, the resultant public scandal would certainly adversely affect his efficiency as a member of this department and tend to destroy the good name of the department itself. He didn't have brains enough to realize it, ignored the warning, lied to his commanding officers and continued to the ruination of his own police career. While the administrators of a police department do not expect its officers to be plaster saints, they are compelled to require a standard of conduct considerably above that exacted by good society of its civilian members.

It would seem safe enough to assume that you have a practical working conception of what constitutes good social conduct or you wouldn't be in the department. Nothing more should be needed to keep you out of trouble. If you have such a conception and bolster it up with a thoroughly understanding study of your rules and regulations and the law which it is your duty to observe and enforce, we should be able to drop the subject with the old "bromidium,"—"Let your conscience be your guide."

However, there is just one more point that we have found it necessary to make in this connection—your responsibility in helping to maintain the good conduct of your fellow officers and thereby the good name and efficiency of the department. During the past fifteen years a queer concept has grown into the minds of the American people, particularly those who have grown into maturity during those years, with respect to everything associated with the term "stool pigeon" or "rat." Newspaper, magazine, movie and novel have romantically played up so-called gang code and loyalty. Publications and pictures have ingrained the belief into growing American youth—and a good many of their elders—that anyone who gives the police any information at all is a "stool pigeon" or "rat." Now it hasn't been so much the fault of the press and the pictures as it has been the peculiar proneness on the part of Americans to misapply terms, slogans, catchwords, policies, practices, and creeds.

A "stool pigeon" or "rat"—the terms are synonymous—is one crook who informs the police of the activities of other crooks, either solely for cash reward or revenge, or police protection for his own nefarious practices. Remember—there are three main elements: first of all, the informant must be a crook; second, those on whom he informs must be crooks; and third, the reason for his informing is grossly selfish.

During the unpopular era of prohibition—and in this the press did, without the slightest shadow of a doubt, play a direct part— the term "rat" or "stool pigeon" was applied to the citizen who informed the police because of a sense of civic duty and to the regularly employed under-cover investigator. The investigator might have had just as high ideals as you; many of them had a firm belief in the hopeless cause for which they were striving, and laid down their lives just as willingly and for the same motives as you would in the defense of your own home against a murderous intruder, but they were branded almost universally with that dread term "rat" or "stool pigeon." With that step taken it was only a little distance for many decent citizens to go on assuming that if they told the police anything they were by that act becoming "rats" or "stool pigeons." Any police officer with a few months experience is familiar with the approach of some good plain, garden-variety citizen, "I suppose I am a 'stool pigeon' but somehow it seems necessary to tell you: I overheard Bill Jones confide to one of his buddies that he stole the watch off that drunk the other night." Apologizing if you please, for giving information which a shred of social conscience should induce him to give without the slightest hesitation! But the poor oaf's mind, like that of so many millions of his fellows, has been warped by the insinuating publications and moving pictures with which he has grown up. And if Bill Jones should happen to be a member of the same school, the same lodge, or even of the same neighborhood, this fellow wouldn't even have considered telling the police about his crime. That kind of mind and conscience distortion is so prevalent that it is one very important reason why the American police have had such hard sledding in post-war and prohibition days—days of the gangster and maudlin sentimentality for which the press and pictures are so largely to blame.

Tragically enough, this feeling still prevails. Why only during this writing, a journalist, whose stuff is consumed along with the toast and coffee at thousands of breakfast tables, seriously criticized a Chief of Police for assigning new recruits, while their identities as policemen are still generally unknown, to the undercover investigation of illicit liquor and narcotics traffic. Before repeal of prohibition—and, mind you, he represents the typical and very large "public opinion"—he was criticizing the police for using outside special investigators, terming them "stool pigeons" and demanding that the police themselves gather their evidence. Imagine, if you can, an honest, uniformed cop, or even one in plain clothes after a few weeks active police work, walking into a bootleg joint and buying a pint of illicit booze! Even now, since repeal of prohibition, while the preserves of legal liquor dealers are being poached upon by the illicit trafficker, this worthy and widely read gentleman of the press reveals to his faithful readers that the Chief of Police has the disgraceful temerity to assign regularly appointed policemen to the investigation of this activity!

It is probable that this ignorant and unhealthy attitude of our people and those who form what passes as their opinions will be corrected, but it will be at least a generation before its effects will completely disappear. Meanwhile, here is the point for which the immediate foregoing is designed to prepare you:

Among the men and women of your department, just as in any other organization of appreciable size, there are those who, in spite of careful selection, will violate the law and disregard the advice of their superiors and the mandates of their rules and regulations. The law and you who are sworn to enforce it cannot be respectors of persons. If information or reliable suspicion comes to you in any way that one of your brother officers, regardless of rank, has, for example, stolen something, accepted a bribe, or seduced a child, your duty is plain: If it is an act which warrants immediate action, it is up to you to arrest that officer; if it is apparently unnecessary to act with such dispatch, you should confidentially report it in writing, through channels, to the Chief of Police. Not only must you act upon or report such instances reported to or discovered by you, but it sometimes becomes necessary for the administrators to assign you to investigate a report that one of your brother officers has allowed himself to become involved in a crime. It is not for you to say who should be assigned to such disagreeable work. There is no reason why one man in the organization should be made responsible for all of it, nor would it be possible for one man, unassisted, to be capable of handling every such situation. Don't put yourself in the position of being a buck-passer by objecting to this or any other legitimate detail.

On all of these points your Rules and Regulations are quite clear: "He shall refrain from discrediting any member of the Department, but it shall be his duty to inform superior officers of any disobedience or violation by police officers of regulations, orders, laws, or ordinances known to him."

There just isn't any way of dodging your responsibility. If you attempt to do so, it is going to be only a question of time until such disobedience necessitates your own dismissal. Again, under another rule, duties: "Failure of patrolmen to report or take proper action in case of any crime, disorder, or other act or condition requiring police attention, shall be regarded as neglect of duty." This order exempts no person and no classes.

"Discipline." General rules: "For the purpose of discipline, members shall be considered always on duty. Any member of the department, regardless of rank, shall be subject to reprimand, suspension from duty, pay deduction, loss of days off, reduction in grade or dismissal from the department according to the nature or aggravation of the offense, for any violation of these rules and regulations and for any of the following causes:" Listed among the causes thereinafter cited is this: "Neglecting to report to proper officer any violation of a rule or order of conduct by another officer which is of the nature to cause the department embarrassment;" and in the very last of this column: "Violation of any criminal law."

Now, keep in mind that every word in these various rules and regulations has important meaning, just as do the laws. For instance, there may be minor infractions of the rules and regulations which are more technical than real. To use a somewhat trivial example, if you see one of your brother officers unnecessarily speeding, you have a technical conflict not only as between the law and your good judgment but as between your rules and regulations and your good judgment. In such a case it might be that you have just gotten through issuing a summons to someone or several persons for the same kind of violation. It should be perfectly easy for you to take the first opportunity to explain to that offending officer that it is not only embarrassing to the department but to you for the offending officer to drive in such a manner when others are being arrested for the offense. Assuming that his speed is not outrageously great, no superior would criticize you for warning the brother officer without making a formal report to your superiors. If, however, the warning were not taken in the proper spirit or if the offending officer persisted in his improper conduct, then you would have no choice but to report. Then it would become something of the nature to cause the department embarrassment.

But certainly in such law violations as stealing in any form, accepting bribe, improper relations with minor children—to take only a few of the many offenses involving moral turpitude—you can't have the right attitude even as an ordinary good citizen, let alone toward your particular duty as an officer, if you fail to report such offenses to your superiors.

Whether you know the violation, as alleged, to have actually occurred, it is your duty to report even the suspicion—your own or that of someone else—in order that a proper investigation can be made. It may be that your brother officer is unjustly accused; if so, a prompt investigation will clear him before it becomes a matter of common gossip or public scandal.

Remember always that you are a part of the department and if you have any self-respect you should jealously guard its good name. When you belong to an honorable organization, esprit-de-corps does not require that you protect the crooks or moral imbeciles in your midst. On the contrary, it directs that you eagerly assist in ridding the organization of its own hazards.

Almost all such instances are tragic because the offender always has some honest members of his family either interested in his own welfare as such or dependent upon him for support. It necessitates a high type of courage, moral integrity and loyalty to the service to assist in ousting a man from a job, and prosecuting him if the offense requires it, when to do so works a hardship on innocent women and children. But you are faced with the same problem whenever you help to send any man to the penitentiary from the civilian ranks. If you can't face that fact, you had better resign before you start. The police department, no more than any other administrative agency of government, is not a pension bureau or a home for the physically, mentally or morally incompetent. Its reasons for being have already been to some extent emphasized to you. There are public and private agencies specifically designed for the purposes of charity. And you may take some consolation in the knowledge that for every man who loses a job through his own misconduct there are hundreds of other good men eager for the opportunity to give value received in making an honest living for their dependents.

As a final word on this topic, and reverting to our real definition of the "stool pigeon:" a "stool pigeon" is one crook who informs the police of the activities of other crooks in return for his own protection, for revenge, or solely for a monetary consideration. Do you as a police officer, in the light of the foregoing discussion, consider that the honest performance of your duties as outlined in the laws and in your rules and regulations will ever rightfully brand you as a "stool pigeon?" If you do, then you must yourself assume that you are a crook and get out, for such an attitude will sooner or later display itself in your conduct and you will be kicked out.

HOW ABOUT THESE NEWSPAPER REPORTERS?

It has frequently been said that the newspapers can make or break any organization or individual member thereof. Like so many other generalities this statement is not entirely correct, but there is just enough truth in it to justify its heading the discussion of your relationship to the press. The statement to be closer to the truth should be amended to read somewhat as follows: "If the conduct of an organization or any of its individual members becomes so inefficient, overbearing, or corrupt that continued existence is no longer justified, then the press, generally speaking, can, will, and should bring the conditions into the public light where steps may be taken for the correction or removal of the objectionable factors." In making such an amended statement, recognition is taken of the fact that in some localities it is not altogether infrequent to find newspapers that are lined up with or directed by unscruplous political factions who have no regard for the welfare of any portion of the community excepting that selfish group which it represents. These scurrilous rags occasionally take advantage of a low ebb in right-minded public conscience and successfully direct it to the ruination of a decent and efficient public official or institution. But we are not dealing with these exceptions in the formulation of general statements.

On the whole—and without exception, it may be said, with respect to your own community—the newspapers, barring occasional political expedience, are earnest supporters of good government and honest and efficient officials, so far as it lies within their power to be.

There are two fundamental considerations which must be taken into account if one is to understand the press. First, a newspaper exists for profit and, like any other corporation or individual operating for profit, must give the customers what they want. To say whether newspapers form public opinion or public opinion forms newspapers is the same as the old question: which came first, the chicken or the egg? Certain it is that no one newspaper, no matter what the personal desires, beliefs or moral and intellectual attitudes of its publisher may be, can give the public the news and editorials that he thinks the readers should get, regardless of what they want or of what other newspapers are giving them. Nothing, short of absolute news monopoly, would enable any one newspaper, operating for profit, to publish only what it wanted to publish.

August Vollmer, America's noted police administrator and university professor, lecturing at the summer session of the University of Hawaii, cited an example which occurred while he was reorganizing the police department of Honolulu. Chief Vollmer pointed out to his friends among the newspapermen that their accounts of bank holdups were encouraging young men to enter this form of crime. He asked them to play down the news of crime, especially in its details of operation. One publisher gave him the answer sufficient for all of them: "We did that one year and lost just $40,000."

So just as long as newspapers are operated for monetary individual profit in a competitive field, just that long are newspapers going to be compelled to play up crime news or any other kind of news that will increase circulation. Any single newspaper or syndicate of newspapers that attempts to do otherwise faces certain financial ruin.

Now the other fundamental consideration which you should have in mind with respect to newspapers is that men and women gather the news, men and women rewrite the news and get it in shape for other men and women to print; and men and women write the editorials; and those men and women are not much different than yourselves. These are facts so obvious to those who have had long contact with newspapermen that it seems childish to dwell upon them. Nevertheless among those of you young men coming into public life are many who have never spoken to a newspaperman. You may be among that large group who have grown up with the impression that a newspaper (or any other printed document) is impersonal, something that is found on your doorstep every day as if placed there by a supernal agency to give you the gospel, dispassionate truth of the world's happenings and thoughts—and that it is true because it is printed. There is a kind of common faith in the printed word among people lacking in experience: "I read it in the paper," or "I read it in a book; therefore, it must be true." You may never have had an opportunity to learn from direct contact or have failed to think for a moment that news is gathered by young men just as human as yourself and almost identical with you in these respects: Both of you are underpaid for the gruelling and difficult assignments which you are given; both of you begin to think, after a few months on the beat, that everybody is against you at one time or another and that nobody can be trusted, with safety. Both of you are to some extent alike in this respect: both of you make investigations and write reports. Both of you are intensely loyal, each to his own profession. But there the similarity ceases.

You are competing against no one but the criminal. The reporter is competing against time and against every other reporter of every other newspaper. You make investigations to ascertain all the unadorned facts and write reports containing all those facts for official purposes. The newspaperman makes investigations to determine all the facts that may have news value and writes them, sometimes ignoring the context from which they were drawn and frequently with raw disregard of their real significance, for entertainment of the newspaper-reading public.

After you are once on the scene of investigation you may work with relative leisure; the newspaperman may only have three or four minutes to get his story in before the paper goes to press. It is usual because of this conflict of situations and objectives for the contact of policeman and reporter to create friction. You arrive at the scene of a murder, let us say, just before a reporter who has been tipped off by one of his informants—they have them just the same as you do. First of all, pending the arrival of the trained investigators, it is your duty to keep everyone, including other policemen, outside the area in which the action leading up to the murder and immediately following it occurred. The newspaperman insists upon getting into the room where the body is lying. He wants to search the personal effects to see if there are any notes, photographs, or other sensational material which will add to the color of his story and thereby to the chances of his own promotion. Both of you are excited. The responsibility of each of you is tremendous. The reporter is insistent upon getting inside the area and you are just as insistent upon keeping him out. If you lose your head and use unnecessary roughness and incivility in accomplishing your purpose, you have probably made an enemy not only of that reporter but of every other newspaperman—not only those of his own paper, but also the others—for, whatever the rivalry among newspapermen may be, give one of them a boot in the breeches, literally or figuratively, and you may just as well have kicked every newspaperman in the city, from the publishers on down to the copy boys, because next to a prima donna, there is probably no person more temperamental than a newspaperman—unless it be a policeman.

The problem is a difficult one for which you can devise nothing but general rules. But, if you understand the problem—and it is the purpose of this discussion to assist you in understanding it— and, assuming you have ordinary intelligence and human sympathy, it is likely that you will handle it satisfactorily. Because, if you understand, you will have the necessary toleration, respect, and calmness of demeanor that will enable you to maintain cordial relations. You will be able to appreciate the newspaperman's task, be able to aid him in accomplishing it, and will find that he, too, will be willing and frequently able to lend you extremely valuable assistance.

You will probably find in the list of general rules of discipline of your Rules and Regulations these proscribed acts with reference to the subject we are now discussing: "Activity as a newspaper correspondent or in furnishing newspapers with information without the consent of the Chief of Police." "Divulgence of any proposed movement of the force or any order or orders received or issued without permission of commanding officer." "Mis-use of police information by giving out that which concerns the business of the department only."

However, these rules must be interpreted according to the spirit rather than the letter. Every one of them, if interpreted literally, would prevent you from giving to newspapermen any information whatever. It is, therefore, necessary to formulate a general rule of interpretation. The only reason which the police department can justify, under the influence of American tradition, for witholding information from the press is when the officers in charge of an investigation believe that the facts, if published, would seriously endanger or delay the successful conclusion of that investigation. All the local reporters have subscribed to the reasonableness of this rule and every one of them supports a "gentlemen's agreement" not to publish anything in a police report which is marked: "No publicity requested until released," signed, timed and dated by a division commander. As long as the reporters honor this agreement, continue to allow them access to virtually every official report.

It is safest for the officers below the rank of sergeant, particularly the newer men, to refer all questions of newspaper reporters regarding investigations to his sergeant. The sergeant, in turn, if uncertain, should refer it to the division commander whose duty it is to decide whether publicity is harmful and if so in his opinion, for the division commander then to make the written request for no publicity. Or, if in the lower ranking officer's opinion, it can safely be immediately released, to give the reporter the desired information or grant authority to his subordinate officers to do so. Such an exception to the rules, however, must be made at the officer's risk and subjects him to disciplinary action if it develops that he has used gross misjudgment or has taken advantage of the liberal interpretation of the rule for an ulterior motive such as personal favoritism toward a particular member of the press.

It must always be kept in mind that no shade of favoritism can be shown in your press dealings. You are courting certain destruction when you do. If you give information to one reporter, upon request, you must give it to all who ask for it. If you volunteer it to one reporter without request, you must make it a point to see that all papers are notified if it is practical to do so. You may find an occasional reporter who will try to make you his special informer. He will shower you with all kinds of blandishments and endeavor to convince you that he will get you promotion or give you publicity favorable to you in various ways. But that very reporter will detest you as a rat if you violate your oath of office and risk your reputation for fair dealing with all. Just as in your official dealings with the general public, you must show no favoritism toward any member of the press. You must show uniform courtesy even though there may come a time when you think, justifiably or not, that one or more of the reporters on the police beat or the papers which they represent are seeking every opportunity to destroy you. Looking at the problem entirely selfishly, if you wish, if you do lose your temper and deliberately and unnecessarily obstruct those against whom you have feelings of dislike, you will furnish them just the opportunity for which they are looking to "dynamite" you and the whole department.

WHAT'S THE USE OF POLICE RECORDS?
HOW DO I USE THEM?

You can never function intelligently as a member of the police organization unless you acquire some understanding of the policies of the department as a whole and the reasons for those policies. Nor can you effectively perform your part in carrying out those policies unless you can see the reasons for the acts which the department and you as an individual officer are called upon to perform. In the beginning of our discussion we touched upon the purposes of the police. Keeping in mind those purposes described as being, fundamentally, the protection of life and the protection of property, we shall attempt to justify modern records systems as means of helping to carry out those purposes.

The functions of a police records system may be grouped under the three main branches: investigation, identification and administration. The records rank in just that order of importance and are built up in just that order of development. We shall, therefore, discuss the system in that order.

Investigation. There are few crimes that are solved and finally disposed of on the day committed or reported to the police. A crime of any consequence frequently requires days, weeks, months, or even years for its solution. The men charged with the investigation of these crimes may each have as many as fifty such cases pending. There is no man living who can keep in mind all the details of just one important case, let alone several dozen. Moreover, it frequently happens that the officer originally assigned to an investigation is relieved of the assignment before its completion, and another officer is assigned. Before finally disposed of, an investigation may be conducted by half a dozen different detectives. As a matter of fact, there is no case of consequence that is not from the outset investigated by more than one man.

Assuming that each man could remember all that he learns, he cannot possibly transmit that information to his associates excepting through written reports; and, without transmitting the information, pooling it so as to round out the whole picture of what happened, where it happened, when it happened, how it happened, and "who in the deed did share," there is no possibility whatever of identifying the criminal, apprehending him, constructing the chain of evidence, and presenting that evidence in an organized body so as to obtain a conviction. It is likely that, without records, offenses reported to the police will be cursorily investigated, remembered for a few days and, without any documentary reminder, dropped from the recollection of the investigators and their supervising heads and the citizen is deprived of the protection for which he is paying you. Whereas, if there is a report of each case to which an officer is assigned, it is possible for a designated officer to follow up every case, facilitate the assistance and supervision of each investigator in the field, and remind him and his superiors if the investigation lags. Every victim of crime can then be assured that before his case is dropped every effort will be made to effect solution.

Identification. One of the first facts which an officer discovers at the beginning of his career is that he almost never arrests an offender in the commission of his first crime. You are safe in assuming that every person that you apprehend for the commission of one crime has committed several others immediately preceding his arrest or during the months and years preceding it. Without adequate department records of offenses and their investigation, it is possible that you may identify, apprehend, and convict a man of one crime—the one which you personally investigated. There may be a hundred other crimes which he has committed in the same fashion, all investigated by different officers and, in the absence of records, those crimes would remain unsolved and officers would be continuing their efforts to solve them when the man who committed them was already serving time in prison.

But, if all the ascertainable facts about every crime are found, recorded, centralized, compared and studied by the man in charge of the detail or division responsible for the investigation of such cases, he will immediately recognize those committed by one man or one gang and, when the perpetrator is apprehended, he has already been identified and as many as a hundred crimes may be solved. That criminal may be sentenced to the penitentiary and, upon release several years later, will go back into the same kind of criminal operation.

Now, without records of his previous operations, he will continue to operate unmolested until again picked up, by accident perhaps; if lucky, the police will convict of one crime and the rest will remain uncleared. Moreover, if there were no records, he would go back to the penitentiary without the knowledge of the previous offenses becoming known to the judge or prison board. But, if investigation records containing the modus operandi have been kept and, if fingerprints were taken when first arrested, as soon as that offender begins his second series of operations, by consulting the methods of operation of known criminals it will be immediately discovered as his work; since you have the fingerprints and photographs, descriptions can be immediately broadcast to the men in the field, followed up by detectives and, within a short time, he is in your custody. Check of his fingerprints with those on file identifies him beyond a doubt. The fingerprint and record sheet is tied up with the reports of the crimes previously committed, which in itself tends to induce confession, and, when he is taken before the court for trial or the prison board for determination of sentence, his record as an habitual offender is convincing argument that he should be kept out of circulation as long as the maximum penalties for his misdeeds will allow.

Administration and General. No business can successfully operate over any length of time unless the manager of that business knows its nature, extent of its operations, who among the employees are conducting the various operations and whether they are accomplishing desired results, and at what cost. So it is with a chief of police and his staff of commanding officers. He must know where crime is being committed, what kinds, how much, when, what is being done to prevent it or apprehend and prosecute the guilty, who or what is aiding in preventing that crime or arresting those offenders, and—sometimes even of more importance—who is lying down on the job. Unless every officer submits written reports in a form which will make it possible to refer to them individually and collectively, to evaluate, tabulate and compare them over a short or long period of time, the directing of the department's forces will be merely guess work.

It is true that the chief does not personally look over every individual report; he has subordinate officers assigned to that particular duty. But he does study the daily consolidated report on which is noted the number of offenses, arrests, and casualties for the previous twenty-four hour period compared with the day before, the previous month, and the same month in the preceding year. He also studies monthly summaries and yearly reports, and sometimes has occasion to refer to individual cases—even trivial matters concerning which some outraged citizen directly interviews the chief, making it necessary for the latter to make a personal study of a report, which may be nothing more serious than a minor noise disturbance. He also receives reports from the statistician concerning the number of cases disposed of by each officer. These reports enable him to determine whether any officer is loaded down with too many assignments while others are given too few; he may be thus able to determine not only who is doing superior work, but why; who is doing inferior work and why; thus being able to more intelligently promote and demote or change assignments, without letting bad conditions continue for years on end with some men doing most of the work and getting little credit while others get by with little effort and receive most of the credit.

If the chief has reports, he doesn't have to guess—but remember, though it is important to record negative results during the progress of the investigation, the chief is mainly interested in reports that record successful results and not in those which merely produce fine literary effect.

What has already been said should be enough to justify extensive written reports and other records. But it is difficult for men new in police experience to realize the necessity of keeping the records of matters which they consider of small consequence. Not only with respect to records of seemingly trivial matters but also in regard to the manner of dealing with them, their importance from several standpoints should be emphasized:

First of all, while it may be of relative unimportance to you as compared with a burglary, a complaint concerning a howling dog may be the most important thing in the life of the complainant for a whole week. You will find that some of our most intelligent and prominent citizens make complaints about matters which are trivial and frequently unjustified. Nevertheless, that may be the one direct contact that an influential citizen has with the police department in his entire life. (How many times did you or the members of your family contact the police before you entered the service?) Now if that one complaint is the only one, as it frequently is, in a lifetime, it is the only one by which the complainant may judge the department. If you handle it carelessly, discourteously, or fail to clear it up, then the complainant, judging the whole department by yourself, believes for the rest of his life that the whole department is careless, discourteous, and inefficient. If it is handled in a way that impresses the complainant with your interest in his welfare, then that citizen believes that the whole department is, in truth, a faithful servant of the people. Remember that his contact with the police makes conversation in his family and among his friends for weeks and months—picture the results, whether for good or bad.

The further importance of keeping records of these minor complaints lies mainly in the fact that they frequently require as much officer-time as the more important cases; certainly taken as a whole they do, for most of the time of the patrol division is taken up with them. Unless they are recorded, at least two-thirds of the department's work is unaccounted for—at least two-thirds of the way you spend your time is unaccounted for. You might be busy continuously on your beat and, if such things were not recorded, there would be not a single thing by which your existence could be justified or your efficiency judged by your superiors; because they can't go around with you in the performance of very much of your official activity and make their own direct observations.

It may be that your beat load is too heavy for one man, but, without the records, there is not a way of proving it to the department's administrators; and, instead of being given assistance, you might very well be given additional burden. Or, suppose it is believed by the administrators that the department should have more men or that the men already in the department are entitled to more money—as we always believe they are—how are the administrators going to prove those facts to the individuals and organizations to whose support or official position we must look for those additional men or that additional pay? Purely from a selfish point of view, if from no other, this should illustrate to you the importance of records.

Moreover, keeping in mind that every complaint is indexed in the records division alphabetically by the names of the victims, offenders, and informants and geographically by street location, these complaints could not be so indexed unless there are reports from which to obtain the information.

This may suggest to you the question: Why index? The answer is obvious in many respects: You frequently have to refer to an old report of an investigation which is resumed. If you remember the name of one of the persons intimately involved or the location, it requires but a minute to find one of the index cards and from that obtain the number of the report, which is filed in its numerical order and therefore easily located within another minute or two. Not only may you thus quickly locate one report but all the reports with which a given individual has been connected since the record system was established.

Again, suppose you are assigned to a new beat—and changes in beats are frequent—you know no one to whom you can go among the residents of that beat for assistance. You will learn very early that your success depends upon the information furnished by residents on your beat or by those who frequent it. Suppose, further, that you are assigned to an important case requiring such assistance. It is quite likely that by consulting the geographical index file you will find someone in the very block or even next door to the seat of the trouble which you are investigating who has been a friend of your predecessor by reason of the latter's service to him. You can be confident that the previous complainant will give you every assistance within his power.

HOW DO I CONDUCT MY INVESTIGATIONS AND
HOW DO I WRITE MY REPORTS?

The one general rule for good reports can be no better expressed than by repeating the quotation from Hans Gross, already cited:

Who, what, where, with what, why, how, when? . . .
What was the crime, who did it, when was it done and where,
How done, and with what motive, who in the deed did share?"

Any report which contains the complete answers to all of these questions is a good report of a good investigation. The only thing that need be added concerns witnesses: Who are they? What is their occupation and general educational and experience background? Exactly what does each claim to have observed and how? Where situated with respect to the location of the crime? With what means, natural or artificial, were they able to observe what they claim to have observed? Why did they observe what they did? What was the time of their observance and how strong were the impressions that they received? How can they fix the time? Cite facts that may tend to show whether a witness is reliable or unreliable, such as age, sex, occupation, education, apparent intelligence, veracity, and willingness to testify.

You will develop your own style and order of presenting the fact and the style and order does not make much difference as long as you intelligently express the facts so that any other officer may know all the essentials that you know. Think of your reports not only as a memorandum for refreshing your own memory but as a means of permanently recording all the pertinent facts so that, if you should die that day or be relieved of the assignment, anyone who is thereafter interested may, by reading your report, know as much about the case as you do. You need hardly be reminded that you can't remember the details and have them included in your report unless you make extensive notes at the time of your investigation.

Brevity may be the "soul of wit" but it is of limited value as the motto for successful police investigation and report writing. We are not thinking now of the small case which is promptly cleaned up and in which the detailed steps are of interest to no one—it may be sufficient to state the nature of the offense, the names and addresses of the complainant and offender, time and place of occurrence, disposition, and the statement that the disposition is known to complainant and offender. But in all cases which are not immediately solved and which may require a long time for solution, it is almost impossible to include in your report too many facts, even though they have seemingly remote bearing on the case. There is no one who can tell at the outset of a major investigation which information is important and which is not. If it were possible to do so, anyone could become a successful investigator. The annals of important investigation by the experts in every department are full of instances to prove this assertion and we shall not go into the citing of them here.

Interrogation of Witnesses. Neither can we, in a brief discussion of report writing and records, discuss at great length the technique of investigation, but by all means keep in mind that even those who can and want to give you valuable information will not do so unless you draw it out by skillful interrogation. Suppose a businessman reports that one of his employees has absconded with the company's funds. Now don't merely dash up and begin and end your investigation by asking if he knows where the culprit is now located. The chances are if he did know he wouldn't be calling upon the police at all. It is almost as useless to merely ask, "Do you have any information by which we might be able to locate him?" because it is surprising to discover how often the reply to this question will also be, "No."

It is well to allow the informant to tell his own story without prompting or direct questioning; and, thereafter, without leading or suggesting, you may ask direct and specific and detailed questions bearing upon everything that the employer knows about his employee. Everything bearing upon his recent activities does not always give you the clue by which to locate him. In that case it is best to go back to the very beginning when that employer first had knowledge of that employee. You must go even beyond that time and ascertain from the references which the employee gave upon entering his service when they first came to know him, where, and under what circumstances. Get the names of all others whom the informant believes may have known the offender, and bring all of it down to the present by getting as much as is ascertainable concerning the offender's friends, acquaintances, fraternal connections, employment, business and professional men with whom he has transacted affairs—even as to where he got his hair cut and his shoes shined, where he spent his vacations and holidays. And, when you have collected all that material, it is then only a matter of checking up on each lead.

Everyone is a product of his past life. What he does in the future is pretty largely regulated by what he did in his past. Somewhere along his future path he will cross one of his old trails. That is the reason why it is truthfully said, "If you know for whom you are looking, it is absolutely certain that you can apprehend him, given the time and the money to continuously follow up." But you never know until the man is actually in your custody just which little bit of the mass of information that you may have collected will furnish the clue that effects the arrest or discloses additional evidence.

Be careful in your reports to state first of all the facts and label them as such. Your opinion in the way of interpreting the facts is important but it should be reserved until the last and labeled as such. By *Facts* we mean not only those things which are supported by your own evidence. You can state as a fact, for instance, that John Jones told you, "I saw Bill Brown with his right fist strike James Smith in the left eye." Whether that is true or not, it is certainly true that John Jones made that statement. Which suggests another reminder that should be mentioned in passing—always state who was present when the observation or statement was made, because you will sooner or later learn the value and meaning of that much of all that is implied by the term, *Corroboration*.

Interrogation of Suspects. The technique of obtaining information from the defendant himself is too large a subject with which to deal here. You can acquire some of it by the readings already recommended. You can do no better than to study the verbatim statements taken from defendents by skilled detectives and by studying the transcripts of stenographic records of examinations conducted by skilled trial lawyers. If you wish to do so in your spare time, you are at liberty to work with and observe the methods employed by experienced detectives in the department. You will thereby learn much that can be learned from no written documents, because the formal statements incriminating a defendent usually follow persuasive discussion which is not recorded. Even assuming it were possible to record every word that is spoken in the examination of a suspect, you would miss the vital factors of attitude, tone of voice, locale and circumstance under which the examination was conducted.

It is well, however, to mention here—because you will find little discussion of them elsewhere in publications by policemen—the interrogation of suspects, some of the things you should not do as a matter of policy, particularly with reference to the obtaining of confessions. Two books, *Our Lawless Police* and *The Third Degree* will indicate to you the necessity of covering this point in discussion of the recruit's problems.

Never lie in any of your work nor use physical violence beyond that justified by law and necessity in defending lives and property in effecting arrest when all other methods fail. Especially never lie nor use physical violence when attempting to obtain confessions. If you are not impressed by the moral and legal prohibitions against such actions, then accept the word of the more intelligent investigators who speak from the knowledge of lifetime experience that, in the long run, you will lose more convictions than you will win if you ignore the advice just given.

With respect to lying, just as soon as you lie about your knowledge of the crime and the suspect knows that you are lying, you, instead of he, are on the defensive. He knows immediately that you have taken a long shot and missed and that all he needs to do is sit tight and keep his mouth shut. If you lie with respect to a promise that you will do something which you know you cannot or will not do, you may clean up that one case but your reputation as a liar and double-crosser will spread so rapidly that never again will you receive that confidence and respect that it is so necessary to receive—even from the underworld. You are not bound, either from the standpoint of good judgment or ethics, to correct a misinterpretation in the mind of a suspect. As long as you stay within the truth, it is quite all right—if you think it desirable—for the suspect to form any conclusions that he wishes.

You are not morally or legally bound to warn him that anything he says may be used against him. Under the laws of this country a confession is still admissable even though the defendant has not been warned; and, as a matter of practice, the prosecuting attorneys prefer that no such warning be given, or, if given, they prefer that it not be recorded in the written statement. Sometimes it has seemed good tactics to impress the suspect with your fairness by pointing out to him that you can make no promises and that whatever he has to say can and may be used against him—or for him, as evidence of his contrition and willingness to make amends as far as he can by assisting the forces of law in clearing up his own misdeeds, thereby meriting some consideration of leniency. Be careful, however, that you do not give him definite assurance that it is better for him to make this or that statement, since such positive assurance has sometimes induced courts to disallow the introduction as evidence of confessions thus obtained.

There is no short-cut to arriving at the truth or falsity of a suspect's story. You must first obtain all the facts that are ascertainable by your own observation and statements of others and thereby be in a position to check his veracity without much difficulty and with or without some of the more scientific aids such as the various types of so-called "lie-detectors," the effective use of which requires an experienced operator and considerable knowledge of the facts.

The Third Degree. Ignorant, brutal, socially unintelligent and lazy policemen, in the past and still to some extent in most departments, employ the so-called "third degree." Right here you should be straightened out on your conception of what constitutes the "third degree," which term strikes horror and righteous indignation into the minds of all right-thinking people. Unfortunately, many of those citizens have assumed that just ordinary severe and justified grilling of a suspect is "third degree." Of course inconvenience and anxiety are by-products of the arrest and questioning of any person. Sometimes the grilling may require several hours on end or several hours on each of two or more successive days. There is no way of avoiding it. There is no reason why it should be avoided. Obviously, if you don't arouse in the suspect's mind considerable discomfort and anxiety, you are not getting anywhere with your interrogation. You will hear many a fond mother complain that her darling boy was held at the police station and put through the "third degree." (The "third degree" simply means physical abuse by means of striking, kicking, or pinching, or any way of inflicting direct physical torture, for the purpose of extorting information and has no place in civilized society from a moral, legal or practical standpoint.) Upon looking into such complaints you almost invariably find that what the mother means is merely that her boy was brought to the police station and questioned. Then it is your job to convince her that what you have done is necessary and that it is not the horrible "third degree."

As in so many other phases of your work, you will profit by studying the case from the other fellow's viewpoint. Assume, for instance, that you are the suspect, whether guilty or innocent, that you are taken into a room where you are shut off from the sight and sound of the rest of the world—no one to defend you but yourself, locked and barred and probably handcuffed without even a desperate fighting chance, surrounded by burly detectives standing or sitting near you with blackjacks, pieces of rubber hose, brass knuckles or even just bare, heavy fists. To one of their questions you give an answer which is not the one they want or expect, whether true or false. A blackjack thuds against your knuckles, your arm, your neck, or even leaves its bloody welt across your cheek—it can always be said you resisted arrest. Or a hard fist crashes against your jaw, or a heavy-shod foot cracks your shin or testicles. After you have suffered a few such agonies and unless your courage is made of steel, you are going to figure out what they want you to say and say it, whether true or false.

Imagine, under similar conditions, 200 pounds of brute "detective" picking up a little man weighing less than 130 pounds, standing him on his feet and knocking him clear across a room where he is picked up by another badge-bearing gorilla and smashed back to the floor in the opposite corner—that is only one of many such occurrences in some departments in years gone by and related not only by victims but by officers who witnessed it, or participated in it. There are men walking the streets today who bear the marks of permanent disfigurement from such felonious assault. (Sadly enough, there are a few men now in some departments who secretly approve of such methods.)

Now, first of all, if you get a confession under such circumstances you cannot be sure that it is true—almost anyone will say anything to avoid further physical punishment of that type, sometimes thinking that he can dodge the consequences later or perhaps convince a jury or judge that he has falsely confessed because of the torture. It may be that he will be afraid when he gets into court to mention the torture and not attempt to disavow his confession and you therefore get a conviction. But you can't be sure you have convicted the right man; and, if you have, every particle of respect for law and society has been beaten out of him—irretrievably lost. If there is any manhood left in him, he will kill you if just a fair opportunity is presented. He will seek every chance to wreak his vengeance on organized society. Can you blame him? Would you feel any differently in his position?

The gross prevalence of crime despite the continued and widespread use of third degree methods should prove that these methods have not been effective. Anthony M. Turano in his article "The Brutalities of the Police" in the July, 1934, *American Mercury*, succinctly expresses this truth when he says, "The increase in criminality in all sections of the republic ought to be sufficient proof that in stooping to conquer, the police have only succeeded in simply stooping."

Even though you clear a few cases by making a beast of yourself and the criminal, have you done anything to protect society? On the contrary you have increased the community's peril. Much better to lose a case or 10,000 cases than to debauch yourself, to debauch another human being, finally, to debauch society. At best, third-degree methods are those of the lazy incompetent; at their worst they mark the depravity of the damned.

RECORD FORMS AND PROCEDURE

You are urged to study *Police Record Systems* by O. W. Wilson and *Police Planning* by the same author. Both volumes are very complete and carefully illustrate the importance of Reports and Records. As you have already learned, reports of crimes and other occurrences are made on specially designed forms. These cases should be entered in abbreviated form on a daily bulletin, the purpose of which is to provide a brief, chronological record of the whole day's transactions for the entire department, for ready reference purposes such as enabling the officers to obtain the numbers given to their cases. It also gives the chief and division heads a brief picture of what is going on and familiarizes all officers with crime occurring on beats and watches other than their own.

The general rule guiding the desk and dispatch officers in determining whether a numbered report shall be made is this: If the matter reported requires the assignment of an officer, then a numbered report should be made. In addition to that, of course, matters not investigated are entered on numbered reports merely for record. To the general rule there are exceptions such as the assignment of officers to the scenes of fires and temporary traffic jams, of which no numbered reports are made. A record of these minor assignments should be kept on blanket, un-numbered monthly reports, the main purpose of which is to account for the considerable time spent in such activities, which would not otherwise be accounted for, and to guarantee that if something more important should develop later, there is some record with which to start the investigation.

Original or Master Report. The *original* or *offense* or *master* or *crime* reports, as they are variously called, are designed to record the first facts reported concerning an offense or occurrence. They are the documentary basis on which to build the record of the investigation in the form of supplementary reports as the investigation develops. Of course, if all the facts sufficient to close the case are immediately submitted, nothing but the original is required. If the case requires additional reports, the latter are attached by the bureau clerks first to the outside of the original in order to bring them to the attention of the report review clerk who, when he has noted their contents, staples them to the back of the original and it is again ready for filing; meanwhile, if still pending, appropriate notations are made in his follow-up system or necessary instructions sent to other officers.

These original forms are more or less standard and similar in that they contain space in which to record, in brief, the who, what, where, when, why, and how. Usually they are made out by one of the officers in the dispatch room as soon as possible after the complaint is first received. If, however, the report is received first by someone outside the dispatch room, it is usually made up by that officer or someone under his direction and forwarded to the dispatch room, where it receives a serial number and is entered on the Bulletin just as in the case of those originating in the dispatch room. The purpose of making out the original as soon as possible is to provide some means of following up the case from its very inception. When a report is numbered and entered on the bulletin, the follow-up system makes it virtually impossible for that case to be lost sight of from the very start and as long as it is pending.

What Is The Modus Operandi Report? This is probably the most commonly used police report. This report should be made for every crime for gain, i.e., larceny, burglary, robbery, fictitious checks, embezzlement, OMFP, OGFP, etc. "Modus operandi" is a Latin term used by Major Atcherley, the English police administrator who popularized the system, and may be interpreted as "manner or method of operation." The system operates upon the principle, well-known to experienced police officers, that every habitual criminal has habitual methods which he applies to every job. After having operated some time, these habits are pretty well fixed. They are formed more or less by accident, as are most habits, but nevertheless they become typical; and, if every case is thoroughly investigated, the trained investigator will be able to determine which among a group of burglaries are committed by the same man or gang.

Usually, for instance, a store burglar will operate only on stores—frequently only on a certain type of store. A burglar may operate usually on certain days of the week and certain times of the day as a result of his belief as to when escape from detection is most likely. He may choose stores operated by people of a certain race who may have peculiar methods of handling their business or money, which he believes offers him the best opportunity or opportunities for escape. He may always enter a rear door or a side window, or at some other particular place, for a variety of reasons—perhaps for none other than that, in his first successful job, entry was effected through a certain point of the building and therefore, without any particular thought, follows the same procedure thereafter. He may, and usually does, use the same instrument or kind of instruments on each job, again either through accidental factor or having used them successfully on his first jobs, or through belief that they are better adapted to his particular kind of breaking in, or through ease of concealment while going to and from the scene, or through sentimental or superstitious belief as to their luck-bringing qualities.

All burglars, of course, will take money; but some burglars look only for money. Others may take only money and jewelry or jewelry of a particular kind for which they have a means of safe and profitable disposal. Others may specialize in certain merchandise such as cigarettes, if they have a good market for them. Usually, when a burglar specializes in loot other than money, the articles which he picks out indicate that he has a good market for them, or for that particular material and this in itself furnishes a clue which may lead to his apprehension through watching places at which such goods are likely to be sold.

In addition to peculiarities with respect to time, person, place attacked, place of entry, instrument used, and choice of loot, there are peculiarities which are termed *trademarks*. The nature of the trademarks may be generally indicated as being those things which are not necessary to the commission of the crime. For instance, every burglar has to choose some particular time, some particular building, building operated by some type of person, and entered at some place with some kind of instrument, and with some object in view; but there are always little peculiarities which are not thus essential to the job, which we call *trademarks*. Suggestive of this sort of thing, we will mention only a few: removing a safe to back store-room and leaving a dummy in its place; pulling down window shades; barricading door to delay officers' entry if discovered; eating food on premises; leaving cigar ashes; spitting tobacco juice; in case of a residence burglary, he may dump all the dresser drawers out on the bed or search them carefully and leave remaining contents undisturbed; cutting light wires; unscrewing light globes; cutting telephone wires; malicious injury to premises; committing of nuisances such as defecating on floor; leaving fabric marks of a certain type of glove, or the sole mark of a certain type of shoe, or the imprint of a bare foot, or stockinged foot. Almost always a diligent search will disclose some peculiarity not a part of some other element of the Modus Operandi, which was not necessary for the commission of the job. These little trademarks may be enough to establish the identity of the individual or at least identify a great number of jobs as being committed by the same man or gang.

Now, taking up each part of the form, the explanation of which has not already been described in discussing other forms:

Under *Date Committed* should be noted not only the date but the day of the week. *Time Committed* is the hour, if known, or the hours between which the offense could have occurred.

The rest of the items will vary with respect to the different crimes for the reporting of which this form is used.

In passing, a word of explanation may be in order as to why this form was designed in its present form. Were it not for the factor of expense, it would be better perhaps, to design a form for each particular type of crime for gain: one form for larceny, another for burglary, another for trick and device, another for forgery, another for embezzlement. However, taking into account the expense factor, and also that many of the elements are the same for all offenses, this form was designed to make it applicable to all crimes for gain. Explanation, therefore, is in order in discussing its use with respect to each of them. In its present set-up it more particularly fits the need of a Burglary Modus Operandi form. As a matter of fact, it is in burglary that the form is probably most useful.

Burglary M.O.: *Person attacked* applies to the person actually in charge of the building, whether residence or store or office, at the time of commission of the burglary; or, in the case of an unoccupied building, the person last or ordinarily in charge. There are four factors to be stated under this item: sex, racial extraction, whether juvenile or adult, and occupation. You do not repeat the name, because that is already noted under victim.

Even where the type of person attacked furnishes no clue as to the identity of the offender, there is one other value or potential value of this information which may enable you to obtain it with better grace: From a larger social point of view it may be valuable, in the course of years, to know what classes in the community suffer the most from criminal operations; just as, in the similar manner, it is useful to know the classes from which the criminals come. It may even be possible, having an accumulation of such information, for a trained statistician to roughly predict what the future crime situation will be as social conditions vary, thus enabling police administrators to organize their forces accordingly.

Property attacked is the type of building entered, for example: One-story, stucco, chain grocery store in outlying district; top-floor dental office in three-story combination store and office building in downtown business district; five room, frame bungalow, vacant lot adjoining.

How committed is the point of entry; for instance, in the case of a dwelling house: rear bedroom window on side adjacent to vacant lot; second-story bathroom at top of outside stairway.

Means of attack is the actual instrument or means by which the entry was effected and it may be almost anything: Unknown hard object, breaking window in top sash at catch; $5/8''$ flat, straight-edged, red painted jimmy, applied as pry between sash and sill directly under center of sash lift; climbing through open window from adjacent tree; unknown, probably pass key on Corbin lock of front door.

Object of attack: type of article stolen, such as: money only; money and men's clothing; cigarettes only; valuable jewelry, etc. This item may be filled in even though nothing is actually taken as in a case where articles are piled up or boxed preparatory to removal and it appears that burglar was frightened away before completing his purpose.

Trademark: See previous discussion.

Larceny: In larceny the elements will be somewhat different; using theft of articles from an automobile parked on street, let us say, parcels from a locked sedan parked on Fourth Street near University: *Where committed—*give the side of street and the number directly in front of which car was parked. *Time committed—*when exact time is not known, the hours between which the theft occurred. The victim may have known that she left wrapped parcels of valuable merchandise, bought at "Sample Store" on the back seat of her locked sedan at 10 a.m. and theft was not discovered until she returned at 12:30 p.m. The time committed is between 10 a.m. and 12:30 p.m.

Person attacked refers to the owner of the thing stolen.

Property attacked is the automobile: 1952 Ford fourdoor locked sedan.

How committed: breaking rear door lock, street side, with unknown instrument, probably pipe.

Object of attack: miscellaneous valuable parcels, mostly expensive dresses and lingerie.

Trademark: This may be difficult to ascertain. Using the same example, here are things you may find or justifiably suspect: Uses automobile and confederate, takes only valuable wrapped parcels from among cheap ones; takes both small and large valuable parcels. With just this information it is safe to conclude the following with respect to the thief's activities: He, with at least one confederate, operates in an automobile which is driven along the parked rows of shoppers' cars; stops alongside of complainant's car, gets out, quickly applies iron pipe to handle and breaks lock; reaches in and gets selected parcels which he throws into their own car. He probably has watched the customer buy the articles and knows what is wrapped in the bundles—otherwise he would not be able to discriminate among them. The probability of the use of the car is further borne out by the fact that some of the parcels would be too large to safely carry away in the arms. Having made these conclusions, you may find upon questioning someone in the immediate vicinity that a car of a certain description was seen in the vicinity and double-parked alongside the victim's car.

Keeping in mind the fact that the perpetrator was able to discriminate among the several parcels in the car, it is safe to assume that as soon as he saw them deposited in the victim's car he signalled to his confederate who probably had his car within sight, who thereupon drove into position. By learning the place at which the articles were purchased, you know where the thief is hanging out to observe purchases and to follow shoppers to their cars. It may be that we find, through the study of the M.O. of similar cases, that there are many such cases bearing the same M.O. We may find that all of them are committed on paydays, or Saturdays, or days on which special sales are carried on in the stores or on any days when the streets in affected areas are crowded, thus affording a lesser chance of detection. Knowing these facts, it is a relatively simple matter to place men in plain-clothes in concealed positions where they can watch all parts of the affected area on the days and during the periods at which the thieves operate and it is certain that within a few days at the most you will have ended your two-man "crime wave."

After arrest the rest is simple. Your M.O.'s have already told you the cases for which they are responsible, you have the complete lists of property, and, upon being confronted with your astounding knowledge of their operations it is probable that they will promptly confess and aid you in recovering stolen loot or informing you of its manner of disposal. You may then find that you have uncovered a fence who has been accepting stolen goods not only from these boys but from several burglars and thieves; and, perhaps before you are through you will have cleaned up other gangs and many other cases not related at all to the relatively small and trivial theft from an automobile with which you started.

All of the foregoing discussion is not mere theorizing; it is based upon actual experience and is typical of what can be done with complete and accurate investigation, reported with equal completeness and accuracy in the M.O. report. Does it convince you of the value of careful investigation and reporting of even thefts which, considered individually, you might otherwise believe too trivial to merit your best efforts? Of course, it may be a year or more before such chain of larcenies are developed. You may have written hundreds of M.O.'s which netted no results, but just one out of hundreds is all that is necessary to set off almost an endless chain of disclosures for as much as a year with respect to major crime.

Watch the Daily Report for the several days or weeks following the apprehension of a gang of juvenile petty thieves—you will invariably note a distinct falling off in the number of larcenies dating from the day of their arrest. Get in the habit of studying this Daily Report which compares the crime record of today with yesterday, this month with last month to date, and with the corresponding month of last year. It will give you more interest in your job and added incentive to do your part in continually reducing the number of crimes and increasing the number of persons charged with those crimes, in current periods as compared with the previous, thereby convincing your officials and the public that you are doing more and better work with fewer men and are therefore entitled to more pay.

You will find suggestions as to what factors constitute the various elements of the M.O. on file in the statisticians code. It is based upon long actual experience and covers most of the situations with respect to the manner of the commission of all crimes for gain. It must not be considered exhaustive, however, for there is frequently something new and unusual cropping up— it is this unusual factor that is particularly valuable.

Listing of property: In the M.O., as in any report necessitating the listing of property, always numerically identify it in one-two-three order. Among a miscellaneous list, the most valuable and identifiable should come first in the list and in each individual description the same rule should be applied; that is, first, in capital letters, the term describing the type of article, followed by sub-type, trade name, general quality or appearance, numbers, initials, or other identifying marks. For example:

1. WRIST WATCH, Man's, Hamilton, white 14 karat gold (list as white metal, when listing in receipt of any kind) movement No. 2734006, Case No. 2536794, rectangular in shape about one inch by three-quarters, attached to wrist band of flat white metal links, cost new three years ago $75. . . . . $ 50.00

2. CAMERA, Leica, F-3 lens, serial number 76831, recently bought new. 150.00

3. RING, Man's, 16 karat white gold, flat band, monogram "P D Q" inlaid green gold in square onyx setting 50.00

4. SILVERWARE, Six each, knives, forks and spoons solid sterling silver, knives stainless steel, Louis XIV Pattern:

6 spoons	@ $5.	$30.00
6 forks	@ $5.	30.00
6 knives	@ $4.	24.00

84.00

5. SUITCASE, men's, tan cowhide, trademark "Gibraltar" stamped on bottom center; heavy brass fittings; corbin lock; initials "PDQ" stamped on upper edge near lock; double hand grips; 12 x 24 x 36 inches; bought new at McInery's six months ago for $50.00 . . . . 35.00

$369.00

In reporting lost, found, or stolen property always give some value to each article. One of the ways in which the efficiency of the department is indicated is by the amount of property recovered compared with that reported lost or stolen. This is not a very exact criterion because values are difficult to set up. However, as long as approximately accurate values are given the articles and, when recovered, are noted in our reports as of the same values given them when reported lost or stolen, the percentages of recovery are approximated and, while only a fair indication, to some extent it does measure the department's yearly efficiency in recovering property as compared with previous years. If a watch when reported stolen is valued at twenty dollars, nevertheless twenty dollars should be the value on report of recovery—one hundred percent recovery.

There is only one fair standard for estimating value—what would the victim have to pay to replace the lost or stolen article at the time of its loss or theft and in its then existing condition? Not what the cost price new might be nor what extrinsic value the victim might place upon it, but what the same kind of article would cost the victim at the time of the loss in the markets available to him. Thus a watch stolen from a retail customer who had just bought it from a jeweler, the price would be what he paid the jeweler (assuming that it was a fair, standard retail price) which might be $35.00. Assuming that the watch was a year old, you would estimate the price on the basis of what the owner would have to pay in the retail market for a secondhand watch of the same make, type and condition which, in this instance, might be twenty dollars. Don't worry too much about the exactitude of your evaluation, but use the guide just given to the best of your knowledge and belief.

There is, however, one condition necessitating exactitude in evaluation. The value in the case of a stolen article taken by larceny determines whether the larceny is of the first or second degree—felony or misdemeanor. For instance, in the case of an article of value approximating two hundred dollars there would be real need of determining its actual worth because Grand Larceny of property exceeding $200 in value carries a penitentiary sentence of not more than ten years; whereas all other larceny, i.e., of property valued at less than $200 is petite larceny, carrying a jail sentence of not more than one year.

In the case of property which has neither been lost, stolen, nor found, but which is held merely for evidence, we cannot credit ourselves with any recovery and consequently no value need be placed on the article in evidence unless it is a means of helping to identify it.

Supplementary Reports. The supplementary report presents few difficulties in usage or form. It is used whenever supplementary information is to be submitted after the writing of the original report, or at the time of the writing of the original report is used by those officers other than the man who makes out the original. Unless two men are working regularly in pairs, as in the detective division, it is better for each to write an individual report of just what he has done and learned, even though he is only one of several working on the same job. The reasons for this requirement are several: If one officer takes the responsibility for writing a report designed to contain information obtained by several in a joint investigation, all pertinent facts will not be included. The officer writing the report will naturally lay emphasis upon his own findings and conclusions and unintentionally tend to minimize or omit the information given him verbally by other officers. The other officers, in turn, will follow the unavoidable tendency to disregard their own responsibility and be too brief in their contributions to the writing of the report. Furthermore, in cases at trial an officer is allowed to refresh his memory from his own report made at the time of the investigation bearing upon the issues then before the court; whereas, officers cannot be allowed to refresh their memories from a report which they did not write. The fact that all the officers contributing to the joint report sign it does not alter its disadvantages. An administrator looking over the reports cannot be certain where the responsibility lies for good or bad work as reflected in the report.

The form of the supplementary is always standard; on the top margin, at least one inch below the edge, the name which heads the original report as the complainant; on the same line in the center of the page, the date when the case was first reported, as shown on the original report; on the same line on the right margin enter the report number. In the cases of crime for gain or other offenses in which the detective division has some responsibility and is therefore to receive a copy of your supplementary, precede the report number with the classification of the offense.

Below this line leave two or three spaces and get right into the recital of facts, keeping in mind what has already been said with reference to investigation and report writing.

If the report extends over more than one page, indicate on each page at the left, immediately below the top line, the number of pages in that particular report and the number of that particular case page.

At the bottom of each page should appear your signature above your name typewritten, followed by your badge number. Then immediately below that enter the date and time of signing the report.

The form of each page would be according to the following example of a three page supplementary report:

JOHN DOE   9-25-52   Burglary 44986
Page 2 of 3 pages
          (Begin body of the report here)
                    (Signature here)
                    Joseph Q. Bush #202
                    10-7-52   1:30 AM

As a general rule, the report should be single-spaced with indented paragraphs of five spaces, and two spaces between paragraphs. However, if it will not require more than one page double-spaced, it is permissible to double-space it as it is a little easier to read and index in double-spaced form. In any investigation of importance more than one sheet will frequently be required and there is no need of using up extra stationery and space in the files by double-spacing.

You may not understand all the reasons for the foregoing requirements of form. The top line is, of course, for ready identification to enable the clerks to attach the loose supplementary to its corresponding original or master report and for the information of others who may be interested in your supplementary before it is attached. The report number, if correct, will easily connect it with the original; but all too frequently the report number is incorrect through transposition of figures or other carelessness, in which case the name of the complainant will enable the clerk to locate the original through the index files. The date of the original report showing in the center of this top line informs the superior officers in checking over your supplementary of the date of the offense or at least when it was reported to the police and, by comparing it with the date of signature of your supplementary, they are able to make necessary conclusions with respect to the progress of the investigation in the absence of the original report. Indicating on each page that page number and the total number of all pages in that particular supplementary immediately announces to the reader the length of the report and enables him to determine whether he has your complete report. The supplementaries, you know, float around through channels for sometimes several hours before being attached to the original and, if the page and total number of pages were not indicated, occassionally one page would seem complete in itself and other pages would remain missing without anyone discovering it. Moreover, if not tied together by page and total number of pages, one page of your three page report might be stapled immediately back of the original, the pages from several other officers' supplementaries following and the rest of your report on the back out of order. The requirement that each page of a multi-paged supplementary be signed and dated is for the same purpose of identification. Otherwise one might read several pages of a supplementary without being sure who had written it or the date when written, and such facts might be vitally important, particularly where identification of the report were necessary in court.

Just as for all other procedure which you are required to follow, there is good reason as just outlined. If you have any doubt at any time that there is good reason for anything you are required to do, your criticism will be welcomed. But first of all ask some superior the reason for the requirement and his explanation will probably satisfy you.

MAKE USE OF THE RECORDS DIVISION

In the foregoing pages you will have found some indication as to the manner in which the Records Division may assist you in your work. Most of you have or will have an opportunity to work one or more days in that division for the purpose of familiarizing yourself with its functions and purposes as the hub of the department's activities.

In addition thereto, it is sufficient to emphasize the value of the identification bureau. At the present time there are on file thousands of photographs of known offenders or suspects who have been arrested by your department, as well as all the records and photographs of all present and former inmates of the State Prison and others who have been arrested in the other counties. There are thousands of fingerprints on file, among which are included many of those arrested in other cities, counties and states, all of those sentenced to the State Prison since, and fingerprint circulars of fugitives. There is a firearms bureau which maintains records of all registered firearms in your state (and all of them are required by law to be registered) indexed according to name of owner, address of owner, and make, type and calibre of gun. But most important to you are the "mug books" containing the photographs and descriptions and charges against all persons who have been photographed by your department.

It is axiomatic that the police officer's success is directly dependent upon his knowledge of known criminals. If you wonder what has made the success of most of the detectives in your department, you will find that they know the known criminals. Not only do they observe them personally but hardly a day goes by without their going through the mug books, studying faces of those who have caused previous trouble and who, therefore, it is safe to assume, are likely to cause trouble in the future. By studying the books the detectives' memories are refreshed with respect to men whom they have arrested and the circumstances recalled may tie up with some investigation in which they are now engaged or are impressed upon the mind so as to immediately be recalled when new cases crop up. By knowing the faces of criminals they recognize them on the streets and places where they congregate and are able to watch their movements and associates and the way they spend time and money. Among many of the persons whom they meet or interrogate almost daily, they recognize persons who have in the past violated the law and thus they are better able to evaluate the information which they seek from such persons.

To increase the value and accessibility of the information concerning known criminals, a file may be established containing special individual records which include photograph, description, name, aliases, address, employment, places frequented, associates, criminal record and M.O. of convicts on parole. These records are filed according to patrol beats in such manner as to enable you in a short time to pick out all those known to have engaged in a particular criminal activity, such as all burglars, for example. You can in the same manner select those of a certain racial extraction. You are required to thoroughly familiarize yourself with all such records of those on your own beat, keep the subjects under inconspicuous surveillance, and report, through your commanding officer, to the Records Division, anything concerning the subject's activities, associates, vehicles used, change of address or employment, etc. After the information has been posted from your report to the criminal record just described, your report is filed under your name and is a valuable means of determining your interest, powers of observation, and general efficiency.

The value of this file depends directly upon your contributions to it so that the information may be kept alive. Conversely, your value depends directly upon the use that you make of the Records Division and the wealth of information which it contains. There are all too few officers using the records. Outside the detective division there are not usually more than half a dozen members of a department who will regularly visit the Records Division, except when called or ordered to appear there.

In the office of the Captain of the Records Division are often kept maps on which are indicated by three month periods the geographical locations of burglaries, larcenies, robberies, and traffic accidents, designated by pins the pattern of which also indicates the watch on which each offense or accident occurred. By studying these maps it is possible for you to get a picture of the whole major crime and accident situation on your beat and for the city as a whole and be able to study the trend, whether increasing or decreasing, from one quarterly period to another. Through the study of these maps you and your field sergeants will be better able to judge how you should distribute your time when patrolling the beat so as to more frequently cover those areas in which crime most frequently occurs. Here, again, there seems to be an absolute disregard of the facilities set up to increase the efficiency of the departments and not many officers regularly study these maps unless required to do so.

Please understand that the whole Records Division is as much for your use as for the use of anyone and you should not feel hesitant about visiting it or any part of it at any time of the day or night. You should be able to study the pictures in the mug books or the maps without permission from anyone. However, if it is desired to consult the files, seek the assistance of anyone of the officers then on duty in the Records Division, all of whom have been instructed to give every possible aid.

A FINAL WORD OF ENCOURAGEMENT

In the foregoing an attempt has been made to hit the high spots of your work and other problems in a manner and to the extent that you may be a little better orientated at the outset of your career. It is hoped that it will be suggestive of the foundation which you yourself must build. Be courageous in the way you tackle the job. Don't be afraid to ask questions when you are uncertain of policy or procedure. In contact with your fellow officers don't hesitate to show your ignorance, especially if it will help you to learn the truth. If anyone laughs at you attribute his attitude to *incurable* ignorance. No one has ever learned much without an inquiring mind. Make every effort to prepare yourself with the knowledge best designed to carry you through the many emergencies in which a lone policeman must make rapid decisions, although emergencies will frequently arise for which no one could possibly have prepared to the exclusion of all uncertainty. If you always delay action until you have proof that you are correct, the march of events will pass you by—if it does not actually run you down.

This statement has often been quoted as great wisdom: "Be sure you are right; then go ahead." Baloney!! or, if you prefer the more recent and even more inelegant equivalent—NERTS!!!

Our old friend, Dr. Gross, again comes to our aid: "Above all it must be well recognized that as nowhere else is it easier to make a mistake, so nowhere should mistakes be more readily pardoned . . . An individual cannot be expected never to make mistakes, but those occupied in criminal matters must be honest and conscientious enough to immediately recognize and freely confess their errors."

May all your mistakes be honest ones and may you never make the same mistake twice.

APPENDIX

A STUDY MANUAL
and
BIBLIOGRAPHY
for
PEACE OFFICERS

By

JOHN P. PEPER, *State Supervisor*
Peace Officers' Training Program

and

FRANK M. BOOLSEN, *Assistant Professor*
Fresno State College

Prepared for use in connection with the
California Peace Officers' Training Program
Basic Peace Officers' Training

Published by the
CALIFORNIA STATE DEPARTMENT OF EDUCATION
Bureau of Trade and Industrial Education
Sacramento

APPENDIX

INTRODUCTION

The material contained herein is a compilation of selected lesson plans developed by California Peace Officers who have received thirty or more hours training in the techniques of teaching and who have been outstanding police instructors.

This manual was developed to serve four purposes:

1. To provide instructional material for the police instructor
2. To provide the student officer with material which can be used effectively to further his advancement in the profession of law enforcement
3. To provide the peace officer with a selected list of references which can be used to increase his knowledge and skill
4. To provide instructional material to the Chief of Police of the small department with a desire for training

The manual is divided into four parts.

Part I   *Classroom Notetaking*

The purpose of this section is to present a practical and simple method of keeping and organizing a classroom notebook.

Part II   *Use of Books by Peace Officers*

The objectives of this section are to indicate: the value to be gained from reading books, how to use a book, and how to read a book.

Part III *Use of the Library by Peace Officers*

The objective of this section is to indicate what library facilities and resources are available to the peace officer in his search for knowledge and information.

71

Part IV   *Bibliography*

The purpose of this section is to provide reference to literature of immediate concern with the police service.

JOHN P. PEPER, Supervisor
Peace Officers' Training

PART I

CLASSROOM NOTETAKING

POLICE TRAINING

Patrol
Unit I—Indoctrination

Topic: Classroom Notetaking

Materials Needed

1. Smith, Samuel and Littlefield, A. S. *Best Methods of Study* (New York, 1946).
2. Levin, Frank K. *How to Read for Self-Improvement* (Chicago, 1947).
3. Sample copy of classroom notes.

Introduction

You have been assigned to this training school for the purpose of obtaining information and learning specific skills that can be utilized by you in your law enforcement work. The success or failure of this school will depend upon your ability to retain this knowledge and use it in the field.

It is practically impossible for anyone to sit in a classroom and absorb all the information which will be presented during the course of the lesson without some organized or systematic method of recording it. Therefore, it is necessary that you learn to take notes—they will represent your written record of learning. The purpose of this discussion is to offer you a practical and simple method of keeping and organizing a notebook. This lesson does not cover the taking of notes in police investigation.

Presentation

I. VALUE OF NOTES
   A. *Good basis for learning.* Frequently, when you listen to a discussion or lecture, the words flow into your ears, but are not always retained or properly digested by

the mind. Notetaking in itself stimulates the mind and tends to hold the interest and attention.

B. **Basis for review.** Newly acquired data may be compared or contrasted with what you already know—by reviewing notes the subject matter is more deeply engraved into your mind. Notes also are invaluable when studying for course tests or civil service examinations.

C. **Permanent record of vital information.** By taking notes you accumulate on paper important ideas that will be of the utmost value in carrying out the duties of a law enforcement agent. They will contain data that will be of value for years to come, and can be used as the basis for establishing a personal library containing material and literature on law enforcement subjects.

D. **Source book for hard-to-find facts.** Such notes represent ready reference material, available at all times for your consideration and study. You can avail yourself of data that has been collected by the instructor from many different sources.

E. **Basis for action.** By study and review of notes, you can firmly imprint in your mind what course of action you should follow when confronted with a non-criminal or criminal problem. The latest techniques and modern methods of handling police problems can always be available in a well-planned and organized notebook.

F. **Written expression.** Taking notes is a practical method of schooling the individual in the technique of written expression in an organized manner of information received.

II. EQUIPMENT

A. *Notebook*

1. *Loose-leaf notebooks are best.* This permits you to organize and reorganize your notes. New and important material may be added; poorly organized notes can be discarded or rewritten. Thus, an officer's notes will always be up-to-date and in correct form.

2. *Size.* 8¹/₂″ × 11″ is the best size to use. This permits use of the recommended size filler paper (8¹/₂″ × 11″). Mimeographed or printed material can be placed directly in the binder without folding.

3. *Binding.* A stiff board binding is recommended. With this type of binder, notes can be written comfortably on table-arm chairs, or on the knee.

B. **Paper.** 8¹/₂″ × 11″, wide-lined and good quality filler paper is the best size and type to use. This size is large enough so that your notes do not become crowded, and it also enables you to underline important detail or to insert notes in the margin.

C. **Writing implements.** A pen is recommended for the following reasons:

1. You should be making a permanent record. Pencil notes become badly smudged and illegible.

2. Ink notes are easier on the eyes and are neater.

3. There is less effort involved. Definite pressure is required on a pencil and this becomes tiresome.

III. OUTLINING

A. Your outline should be brief and concise, but complete enough to form a comprehensive picture of the topic.

B. It is recommended that the following form be used for setting up your notes or outline of the topic being discussed:

Name of Topic:
Chief References and Sources of Data
Date of Lecture or when Material was outlined
(optional)
1. First main heading of the topic.
   a. First significant part related to or supporting I.
      (1) Important item related to A.
         (a) Additional data related to 1.
         (b) Additional data related to 1.
         (c) Et cetera

        (2) Second important idea related to A.
          (a) Additional data related to 2.
          (b) Additional data related to 2.
        (3) Et cetera
    b. Second fact pertaining to main item I.
    c. Et. cetera

2. Second main idea of the topic.
    a. Et cetera
        (1) Et cetera
        (2) Et cetera
          (a) Et cetera
          (b) Et cetera
    b. Et cetera
    c. Et cetera

3. Et cetera

C. The following ideas are set forth to assist you in outlining your lecture notes.

  1. Do not attempt to do the numbering and lettering during the lecture (unless the lecturer writes an outline on the blackboard or otherwise furnishes an outline during the course of the lesson), for the following reasons:

    a. You may lose track of your numbering or lettering and make mistakes.

    b. The writing down of these numbers and letters takes time and effort. It is better to develop attention to the lecture and your general note-taking.

    c. As the lecture further develops, it may be found that you have made a mistake by putting down a minor idea as a major division, and this tends to confuse you.

  2. It is suggested that you do plenty of indenting. Try to indent the main ideas and sub-ideas correctly, without attempting to letter or number them. When the lecture is finished, you should then go back and put in the outline guides.

3. It is also suggested that you leave space between the various ideas, so that when you go back over your notes you may fill in additional ideas which you did not have time to write down during the lecture or which may occur to you after the lecture has been completed.

4. Leave adequate margins at the top and to the left of the notes to permit any additions or corrections.

IV. WHEN AND WHAT NOTES TO TAKE

A. Listen to the instructor, observe his emphasis on an idea. If the speaker has correctly organized his material he will disclose the main factors by stressing certain phrases, the tone of his voice, and repetition of important facts.

B. Watch for important words and terms.

C. Write down the main ideas and sub-ideas during class. Leave extra lines between each idea, then after class you can go back over your notes and fill in additional information.

D. Do not attempt to write down every word during the course of the lecture.

E. As a general rule, dates, amounts, statistical data, examples, and illustrations should be included in your notes.

F. Shorthand notes are not recommended for the following reasons:

1. It is a mechanical process and does not stimulate the mind—the note-taker becomes a robot and loses the value of the lesson.

2. You will fail to remember the lecture or to absorb important subject matter.

3. When shorthand notes become cold, they are difficult to use as reference material.

V. LANGUAGE USAGE AND GENERAL SUGGESTIONS

A. Clarity and brevity are essential for good note-taking. However, your notes should not be so brief that they lose their value and meaning for later reference. Remember, your classroom notes should be taken with the idea of their becoming a permanent record. You should restrict yourself to the essentials so as to avoid a notebook that would assume the size of a large encyclopedia.

B. Employ a simple vocabulary and write in a clear and concise manner. Use simple, complete sentences. Restate the ideas presented in your own words. Eliminate all unnecessary or confusing words.

C. Develop your own system of common abbreviations. You will find that this will be of great value to you in taking notes. However, abbreviate only when there will never be any doubt as to what an abbreviation represents. The following are some common abbreviations that you may find useful: ref. (reference); p. (page); info. (information); Sacto. (Sacramento); *et al.* (and others); & (and); Gov't. (Government); bk. (book); etc (and so forth); e.g. (for example); assoc. (association).

D. Number your pages so that your notes will not become mixed up.

E. Your notebook should be divided into sections by pasting cut-out index tabs in several places so that they will protrude at the margin of the paper and serve as a visible index for a particular subject or topic. Print the name of the topic or subject on each tab. You should keep in one section all notes concerning one topic. The index for each subject should be made at the completion of the particular subject.

F. Do not hesitate to ask the instructor questions. Ask him to clarify any disputed or doubtful points while the ideas are still fresh in everyone's mind. But do not inadvertently interrupt the instructor's train of thought or presentation of an idea. Wait until he has completed his presentation of a particular problem, then ask him to clear up any problem you may have.

G. Try to get in your mind the pattern the lecturer is following—his outline—and your outline will develop much easier.

VI. REVIEW OF NOTES

    A. Review your notes immediately after writing them. This will engrave the subject matter more deeply upon your mind. It will also enable you to retain your mastery of the subject.

    B. Revise your notes before they become cold and add any new information that is pertinent to the subject being studied. The practice of touching up and rounding out notes will make them more valuable for later reference.

    C. Apply your notes to practical problems. Whenever you have been confronted with a difficult problem, consult your notes to see if you can find the solution. If the notes do not reveal the answer, seek out the information in a book or any material that may have been published relative to the particular problem.

Application

The instructor will present a brief lesson to the class and the class will take notes in accordance with the methods as set forth in this unit on notetaking. After completion of the lesson, the notes should be discussed in class. The instructor will then pass out copies of a suggestive outline of the lesson. The officer should compare this outline with his own notes.

APPENDIX A

The following is presented as a sample outline on *The Law of Crime*. It was prepared by the Los Angeles Police Department and is used with their permission.

SAMPLE OUTLINE

Topic: THE LAW OF CRIME

References

Robinton, Walter H.: *Basic Procedure in Law Enforcement* (Gainsville, Florida, University of Florida, 1943.) 140 pp.

Perkins, Rollin M.: *Elements of Police Science* (Chicago, The Foundation Press, Inc., 1942.)   651 pp.
Penal Code of the State of California.
Williams, John B.: *Criminal Law Outline* (Duplicated by and available through the California State Department of Education, Bureau of Trade and Industrial Education, Sacramento, 1951.)

I. SOURCE OF CALIFORNIA LAW

   A. Common Law.
      1. Defined.
      2. Influence on Statutory Law and Judicial Construction.
   B. Statutory Law
      1. Kinds of:
         a. Substantive
         b. Procedural
      2. Sources
         a. Initiative
         b. Legislative enactment
            (1) Acts of Congress
            (2) Acts of State and Local Legislature
            (3) Constitutional Provisions
   C. Judicial Construction
      1. Source
      2. Effect

II. CRIMES IN GENERAL

   A. Definition—P. C. 15.
   B. Elements of a Crime
      1. Act
      2. Intent
         a. Types
            (1) General or Presumed
            (2) Specific
            (3) Constructive or Transferred
            (4) Negligence
         b. Distinction between intent and motive
         c. Intoxication as affecting intent—P. C. 22

C. Corpus Delicti Defined
D. Division of Crimes—P. C. 15
    1. Felony
    2. Misdemeanor
E. Crime and Torts Distinguished

III. PARTIES TO A CRIME

A. Persons capable of committing crimes—P. C. 26
B. Principles and Accessories—P. C. 30
    1. Principle defined—P. C. 31
    2. Accessory defined—P. C. 32
C. Accomplice defined

IV. LAWS OF ARREST

A. Entrapment defined
B. Arrest defined—P. C. 834
C. How an arrest is made—P. C. 835
D. Elements of arrest—P. C. 841 and 834
    1. Intent or purpose to arrest
    2. Reason for arrest
    3. Authority to arrest
    4. Actual or constructive restraint
E. Arrest by peace officers—P. C. 836
F. Arrests by private persons—P. C. 837
G. Use of Force in arresting—P. C. 835
H. Justifiable Homicide—P. C. 196 and 197
I. Breaking in to arrest—P. C. 844 and 845
J. Resisting arrest—P. C. 148
K. Immunities from arrest
    1. Diplomatic Immunity
    2. Foreign Consuls
    3. U. S. Senators and Representatives
    4. State Senators and Representatives
    5. Voters
    6. U. S. Mail

V. ELEMENTS OF COMMON CRIMES

A. Assaults—Misdemeanor
B. Battery

C. Assaults—Felonious
D. Theft
   1. Petty
   2. Grand
   3. Theft of lost property—P. C. 485
E. Burglary
F. Robbery
G. Rape
H. Homicides
   1. Murder
   2. Manslaughter
   3. Justifiable and excusable homicide
I. Disturbing the Peace
J. Vagrancy
K. Other crimes of lesser importance to peace officers
   1. Conspiracy
   2. Extortion
   3. Seduction
   4. Abduction
   5. Other sex crimes
   6. Instructor may enlarge this list to suit.

Test

Practical Test: Application of the Procedure for Notetaking as set forth in this section. An objective type test should be given at the conclusion of the lessons contained in this booklet.

References

Smith, Samual and Littlefield, A. W.: *Best Methods of Study* (New York, Barnes and Noble, Inc., 1946.)

University of Southern California, School of Public Administration, Deliquency Control Institute. *Techniques of Learning and Teaching* (Los Angeles).

Levin, Frank Kern.: *How to Read for Self-Improvement* (Chicago, American Technical Society, 1947.) 246 pp.

PART II

USE OF BOOKS

Topic: Use of Books by Peace Officers

Materials Needed

Levin, Frank K.: *How to Read for Self-Improvement* (Chicago, 1947.)

Headley, Leal A.: *Making the Most of Books* (Chicago, 1932.)

A book on law enforcement

Copies of charts as set forth under section on Application

Copies of recommended bibliography on law enforcement

Introduction

The main purpose of this unit is to state the simple fact that books, periodicals, and other printed material can be used as stepping stones to success. You can obtain self-improvement through reading, and you will find that reading, as such, can be a pleasure and an adventure rather than a tiresome task that must be performed. The objective of this lesson is to point out to you: (1) the value to be gained from reading books; (2) how to use a book; and (3) how to read a book. These tasks are not as simple as they seem. However, the average person, by applying himself, can learn how to use and how to read a book.

Why should you be interested in books? The best answer to this question is probably an example. Each one of you knows that if you were to have your right arm placed in a cast, and then hung in a sling around your neck for six months, a year, or two years, it would be at the end of that time virtually useless. If you didn't exercise it, it would remain that way. Quite probably you will agree, your mind works in the same manner. If you exercise it frequently, it remains active. If you don't exercise it, it becomes inactive. The less you exercise it, the less useful it is to you. The more you exercise it, the more useful it is to you. Simply, then, it would seem that mental exercise is important, and one of the best ways to get it is to develop the habit of regular reading.

Again, much like muscular exercise, it isn't necessary to read at long lengths, but a great deal of value will be obtained if regular reading for reasonable periods is followed.

Presentation

I. VALUE OF BOOKS
   A. To do a good job, you must know how. To know how, you must learn either by practical experience or by the experience of someone else. There is no substitute for personal experience in law enforcement. But practical experience may be gained faster and learned better if you benefit by those things that others have experienced before you.
   B. A second value is based on the fact that all of you should be interested in the opinion of your neighbors. Your place and that of your family in the community, your working condition, and your salary depend upon the kind of job you do as an individual, and as part of an organization. By reading, you facilitate your ability to talk better and with more authority, whether you are handling cases, answering questions, or conversing with friends. Out of self-improvement comes betterment of your personal position in the community.
   C. Another value in the use of books arises from the fact that only fundamentals are taught in the classroom. It is possible in a lecture period to cover only sketchily much of the material, and much of it must be left unsaid. So you must supplement the information that is given in classroom with the reading of your own if you are to gain full value from the subject in which you are interested.
   D. The fourth value of books is that they often can help you solve a problem. You may be actively investigating a case, it may be a bunco case, a series of burglaries, an individual who is mentally unbalanced, or a traffic problem, and perhaps you are having a tough time in obtaining the proper solution. At this point you should stop and consider that probably, someone wrote all he

knew about the subject you are worrying about. All you have to do is to find that material, and profit by it. Probably you can't use all of it, but quite probably, you can apply a good deal of it to your problem.

E.   By reading you can increase your knowledge. In a very practical way, this can be of considerable value to you if you are interested in advancement in the field of law enforcement. In most organizations, promotional examinations are held. Their nature differs in the various departments, but very often the subject matter involves not only information which may be gained from practical experience, but also material of a technical nature. It is, then, that by increasing your knowledge of the field, you would be better qualified to take a promotional examination than if you had given the subject matter no thought before you took the examination.

F.   One word of caution should be mentioned in connection with the reading of books. If you have a reading habit and read considerably, and if you read only books on police subjects, you probably will wind up not only by boring yourself and others, but by knowing only one thing. Although the purpose of this discussion is to emphasize the value of books in law enforcement, you should recognize that reading can be done for the purpose of gathering general information as well as for relaxation, and that you should vary the subject matter.

II.   How to Use a Book

A.   Know what a book has in it. If you are going to read a book, you should first examine the book to find out whether or not you are interested. A book is like a tool. You must know its purpose and know how to use it, then you will get the most out of it. When investigating a crime situation, the efficient law enforcement officer always determines: WHO, WHERE, WHEN, WHAT, WHY and HOW. These same principles can be applied to the initial investigation of a book: Who wrote it? Where and how did the author obtain his

material for the book? When was it written? What
does it contain? Why was it written?

B.   The Organizational Structure of a Book.

  1.   *The title page contains:* the title of the book; the
       name of the author, and sometimes other informa-
       tion about him, such as position held, and aca-
       demic degrees; the publisher; and the place and
       date of publication. A book should be remem-
       bered by these facts, rather than the "one with the
       red cover."

  2.   *The copyright page* appears on the back of the title
       page and here will be found the copyright date.
       It will also indicate when the book was first pub-
       lished and if any subsequent revisions have been
       made.

  3.   *The preface* generally introduces an author to the
       reader and acknowledges any assistance which
       may have been obtained. It may also state the
       purpose of the book and the methods used in
       collecting the data.

  4.   *The introduction* is an important part of nearly
       every book. It provides the author with an oppor-
       tunity to explain the purpose and scope of this
       work. It frequently provides background for the
       author's point of view, his chief assumption, and
       suggestions on how to use the book.

  5.   *The table of contents* lists the parts of the book
       and their order of appearance. The table of con-
       tents will give you a general idea of what the book
       contains. By studying what topics are treated in
       a book, you may save a considerable amount of
       time and effort. If you are seeking information
       on Investigation of Burglary, the table of contents
       will state whether or not the book contains data
       relative to this subject.

  6.   *The list of illustrations* tabulates the maps, charts,
       diagrams, etc., which appear in the text. Modern
       books on law enforcement problems frequently

contain illustrative materials that are extremely useful to an officer and they often effectively express ideas that would otherwise take pages of tedious description.

7. *The text* is the main part of the book—the book proper.

8. *The appendix* contains supplementary material which the author thought best not to incorporate in the main body of the text. It may consist of a list of dates and events, copies of laws, ordinances or constitutions, statistical data or other materials.

9. *A glossary* is a partial dictionary explaining terms or words. Textbooks of a technical nature generally include definitions of terms peculiar to the subject. You should consult the glossary whenever you are doubtful about the meaning of a term. If the book does not have a glossary, consult a dictionary or reference book.

10. *The Reading List* is a list of books, periodicals and other printed material pertaining to the subject matter covered in the book. It is useful as a guide if you are seeking further information on a particular subject.

11. *The index* is an alphabetical list of topics, persons, events, etc., discussed in the book with references to the pages or sections on which each is mentioned. If you are interested in one subject you would save a considerable amount of time by using the index and picking out only those parts of the book which pertain to the subject. An index serves to bring together the information on a certain topic that, because of the plan of the book, had to be placed in different chapters or sections. For example, a book on police procedure may discuss res gestae in relation to different crimes. Consequently, information about res gestae will be found in various sections of the book. The index will tell you where to locate this informa-

tion. For example, if you wanted to learn the definition of res gestae you would look for res gestae in the index. It may be listed as follows:

	Page
Res Gestae	
Defined	40
Use of	41

If you wanted information about the res gestae of burglary, you would probably have to look under burglary:

	Page
Burglary	
Corpus delecti	80
defined	79
modus operandi	81
of railroad cars	85
res gestae	81
with explosives	86

A book on fingerprinting may mention Sir Edward Richard Henry in several places. By referring to the index, you can soon learn all the author has to say about him. For example:

	Page
Henry, Edward R.	10, 15, 88, 141
History of fingerprinting	1–24

Different styles are used by authors in compiling an index. You may have to look under several headings to find the topic in which you are interested. For example, drunkenness may be indexed as alcoholism. Generally, numbers in indexes refer to pages; but in some instances they designate paragraphs or sections of the book. For example, numbers in a penal code index will refer to the penal code section and not to the page where a particular section is located. When this method or any deviation from the normal reference to page numbers is used, the index will contain a brief explanation of the numbering system employed in the book.

12. Note: The make-up of books follows a fairly constant pattern. Few books have all the parts as set forth above. Numerous variations are possible, but most of the items will be found in a book. Therefore, before using a book, consult the table of contents for the parts included in the text and their order of appearance. Become well acquainted with a book before using it.

C. Footnotes and References.

1. You should carefully read all references and footnotes; they cite sources of information, explain a point of view, or refer you to additional material.

2. There are several common methods of making references, marks, or abbreviations which are used in relation to footnotes. They are:

a. *An arabic superior figure* calls attention to a footnote, usually in smaller type, at the bottom of the page, at the end of a chapter, or at the back of the book. For example, "the United States Supreme Court in Jones vs. Scott[2] ruled that—." Asterisks, daggers, or other symbols are generally used with figures. For example, "16% of the 10,000[*] persons arrested had no prior record."

b. *Ibid* means "in the same place" and refers to the reference immediately preceding.

c. *Op. cit.* refers you to the last preceding reference to the book of a particular author. For example, you may read Alphonse Bertillion and find at the bottom of the page "op. cit p. 156." Turn back in the book until you find the footnote reference to the book by Alphonse Bertillion; and you will find the name of the book there. The page number after the words "op. cit." refers to the page in the book written by Alphonse Bertillion.

d. *of. p. 50* refers you to page fifty for further information relative to the topic.

e. *e.g.,* means "for example."

f. *ff.,* means "following."

g. *etc.,* means "and so forth."

h. *i.e.,* means "that is."

i. *p. pp.,* is an abbreviation of "page" and "pages."

j. *viz.,* means "namely."

k. *vol.,* means "volume."

l. *vols.,* means "volumes."

m. *loc cit.,* means "in the place cited;" "in the passage last referred to."

n. *supra,* means "above."

o. *infra,* means "below."

III. READING A BOOK

A. Learning through Reading.

1. A textbook represents organized knowledge which can assist you on the road to self-improvement. Knowledge can make you essential; lack of it can prevent your promotion and advancement to greater opportunities.

2. Reading alone will not guarantee efficiency on the job any more than education assures happiness. However, the well-read person will be able to take advantage of opportunities better than an individual who refuses to improve himself or refuses to overcome any dislike for serious reading. A book is an opportunity to learn.

3. *Learning to read is important. Applying the newly-acquired knowledge is of greater importance. Put the knowledge you acquire to work as you acquire it. Put it to work on the job!*

4. You want to read, but you have no time? *Investigate the use of your time.* How much of it is spent in sleeping, eating, working, recreation, and reading for self-improvement? *Be honest with the analysis of yourself, how much time do you waste?* Where can you put in time for self-improvement reading? Plan your day, set aside certain definite hours each

week for your reading. Proper use of your leisure time can be made to pay dividends.

B. Effective Habits of Study.
   1. Establish habits of thought which help you learn. Be alert, adopt a challenging mental attitude.
      a. How does this tie in with what you already know?
      b. How can you use this information on the job?
      c. Does the author know what he is writing about?
   2. Self-motivation is important. Set a goal for yourself and stick to it. Be eager to learn.
   3. Don't read if you are tired. Relax for about 10 minutes before you start to read.
      a. Take a shower-bath or wash hands and face with cool water before studying. Either one of these methods is very refreshing.
      b. Listening to soft, semi-classical music is also an aid to relaxation. But, turn off the radio when you study!
   4. Read in a well-ventilated room. The room temperature should not be too warm, about 70 degrees Fahrenheit.
   5. Good lighting is very important. Avoid shadows or glare. Overhead light should come over your left shoulder.
   6. If you develop eye weariness or headaches, you should have your eyes examined.
   7. Good posture as you sit is important. Use a comfortable chair, but not too comfortable. Some students prefer to study at a table and sit on a hard chair. This prevents over-relaxation while reading and avoids sleepiness. You must be mentally alert to learn. Interesting reading for self-improvement will not tire you.
   8. Brain work involves the use of muscles just as physical work does—therefore, your mind can be-

come fatigued. Rest a few minutes at the end of each hour of reading. After you have completed your reading, go for a walk. This type of exercise will bring about better blood circulation and aid in the removal of fatigue toxine.

9. Never study immediately after having eaten a heavy meal. Do not study if hungry; satisfy this desire before starting.

10. If possible, carefully select your place of study. It should be quiet and free from distraction.

11. Do not let your mind wander off when you read. Train yourself to call back your mind to the work at hand. Discipline yourself and you can learn to concentrate. Keep your attention fixed on one thing and limit your thoughts to a single definite object.

C. Improving your Reading Habits.

1. Increasing your reading speed.

a. Good readers are fast readers. Poor readers are slow readers. A poor reader may read only 100 to 150 words per minute; a good reader can read from 400 to 600 words per minute. How fast can you read? Read three pages of a book of a non-technical nature. Time yourself. Take the total number of words read, and divide it by the number of minutes. This will give you your reading speed.

b. Do not read so fast that your speed interferes with your retention. A technical book on criminal investigation should be read more deliberately than a light novel. Nevertheless, always read as fast as retention and comprehension will permit.

c. Force yourself to read newspaper or magazine articles, and strive for speed. Be a lively and active reader. If you persistently strive to increase your speed you will find that there is a definite carryover to your reading articles of a technical nature.

2. Do not regress in your reading. Going back and re-reading words or sentences in order to understand them is a bad habit which you must break if you are to improve your reading.

3. Reading word by word is another bad habit possessed by poor readers. You should practice reading phrases or words in their natural groupings and not single words. Reduce the number of fixations, i.e., the number of times your eyes come to rest, to three or five stops per line.

4. When you read, the book should be kept about 14 inches from your eyes.

5. The habit of moving the lips in silent reading is a very bad habit because it slows up reading. Since movement of the lips involves the use of the tongue and vocal chords, it has a tendency to tire a person because there is so much muscular activity. You may cure yourself of lip movement by putting your finger or some other object between your teeth while you read.

6. The auditory reader continually hears the words as he reads them. He does not move his lips, but is always aware of the pronunciation of words. By increasing reading speed and the development of other good reading habits, you can overcome this problem and read with ease and competence.

7. Pointing at words with the finger while reading is a bad habit which can be quickly overcome.

8. Comprehension and retention of what you read can only be attained if you continually and conscientiously strive to improve your reading and studying habits. Speed alone is valueless if it is not accompanied by alertness of mind. You must also understand the meaning of each word you read. If you don't know the definition of a word, look it up in the dictionary before you go ahead.

IV. PLANNED READING

 A. To get the most out of a textbook it is suggested that you adopt a systematic method of reading. Employ a plan best adapted to your needs and to the type of books you are using. Inasmuch as books on law enforcement are non-fiction and technical in relation to treatment of subject matter, it is suggested that you try the following plan:

  1. First Reading—investigate the book as to WHO, WHERE, WHEN, WHAT, WHY and HOW. Then, skim through the book, marking important points. Put a question mark next to statements which seem doubtful, or untrue. Try to grasp the broad basic principles of the text. Do not be concerned or worried about detail. Do not mark books which are not your own.

  2. Second Reading—you should now read the book for detail. This requires a less rapid and more thorough reading. Underline the more important passages and the key facts which you should remember. Check the doubtful statements. Some students prefer to take notes at this time. Be sure you understand the meaning of all words. Consult the glossary or dictionary.

  3. Review Reading—some students prefer to read a book three times. During the third time they correlate the over-all view with the detailed view. Some take notes during this reading. It is not a necessity to read a book three times to grasp its full value and significance. If you have underlined important points and made marginal notes during your second reading, you have grasped the basic fundamentals of the text and it will always serve as a ready reference when needed.

 B. Notetaking and Outlining.

  1. For the mechanics of notetaking and outlining, it is suggested that you consult the lesson on "Classroom

Notetaking." Particularly the sections on equipment and outlining.

2. Do not make these tasks a drudgery.

Application

I. The instructor should bring to class several books and discuss their organization and treatment of subject matter. The following books are suggested:
   A. A book on law enforcement or allied subjects.
   B. *How to Read for Self-Improvement* by Frank K. Levin.
   C. *Making the Most of Books* by Leal A. Headley.

II. USE OF TIME FOR VOCATIONAL READING
   A. Distribute a time chart to the class (or draw one on the blackboard) and have them fill it out to show what they are doing every hour of the day, every day of the week. Analyze several of these charts. In lieu of a printed chart, draw one on the blackboard.
   B. Use a second chart showing each day of the week and the various times one is likely to be wasting time—for example, street car, rest period, lunch period. Discuss the use of these periods to determine if some portion of each could be used for reading purposes.

III. DEVELOPING READING SPEED
   A. Discuss with the class various methods of increasing their reading speed.
   B. Show the class various systems used for improving eye-span. For example:
      1. In the following chart, look at line 1, focus the eyes so that you can see A and B; look at line 2, focus the eyes so that you can see C and D, etc.

A	1	B	C	2	D
E	3	F	G	4	H
I	5	J	K	6	L

2.   Have the class read the following exercise:

The felonious	presence, by
taking and	violence or
carrying away	by placing
of the	him in
personal property	fear of
of another,	violence.
either from	
him or	
in his	

Repeat the exercise, but with a greater eye-span:

The felonious taking	or in his
and carrying away	presence, by violence
of the personal	or by placing
property of another,	him in fear
either from him	of violence

C. Discuss and demonstrate in class methods used to overcome the bad habits of reading, such as, the habit of moving lips while reading, finger pointing, auditory reading, etc.

D. Distribute a recommended reading list to the class.

Test

An objective type test should be given at the conclusion of the lessons contained in this section.

References

See Application I, A, B, & C.

PART III

USE OF THE LIBRARY

Topic: Use of the Library by Peace Officers

Materials Needed

1. Minnesota University, Division of Library Instruction; *The The Use of Books and Libraries.* (Minneapolis, 1937.)
2. Hunt, Peyton, Bibliography and Footnotes. (Berkeley, 1949.)
3. Samples catalog cards.
4. Copies of several of the more useful and popular indexes and reference books.
5. Copies of sample pages from the *Reader's Guide to Periodical Literature.*

Introduction

There are available to peace officers of the State of California several million books in libraries of various types, (the same is true of other states), but it is necessary to know where and how to find these books.

It has been said that the well informed person is not the one who tries to know everything, but that the well informed person is the man who knows where to look or where to go to find out what he wants to know. As an example familiar to all of us: It is impossible for any attorney to carry in his mind all the law on a subject. To be prepared when he goes to court, it is necessary for him to look up references. In the large law firm, often a staff consisting of a number of persons does nothing but look up references for members of the organization who handle the cases in court. In our own business, we know that we are called upon to enforce numerous laws and ordinances, and it would be impossible for us to know the specific provisions of all of them. However, most of us are acquainted with the place to look if we want to know what a particular law specifies or what a particular ordinance requires. The objective of this lesson is to indicate what resources are available in our search for knowledge and information.

Presentation

I. LIBRARIES AVAILABLE
   A. **Departmental Libraries.**
      1. *Police Departments.* Some departments maintain a small library containing publications on technical police subjects. Expansion of such collections would be an excellent opportunity to make available to department personnel the latest books and periodicals on law enforcement and allied subjects.
      2. *City or County Law Libraries.* These facilities are available for use and consultation.
   B. **Public Libraries.**
      1. *City or Municipal Libraries.* There is in every sizeable city in California a free public library, which, depending upon the size of the community, has upon its shelves thousands of books and periodicals, and a smaller collection of pamphlets, maps, globes, pictures, and sometimes phonograph records and films. Large city libraries have branches located in different important neighborhood centers which are distributing agencies. Many books and periodicals of professional interest to the law enforcement officer are to be found in city libraries.
      2. *County Libraries.* Most of the counties in California have a free public library, established by the Board of Supervisors with the main office in the county seat. Branches are established wherever needed throughout the county. While the book collection at any one branch may be small, all residents of the county have access to the collection of books in the main library through the assistant in charge of the branch.
      3. *California State Library.* The State Library at Sacramento has more than 400,000 books for use of the residents of the state. These books, except for a comparatively small group of rare books and

reference tools, may be borrowed by anyone in the state, through his own library. People living in Sacramento may borrow directly from the State Library, and those living in other communities are encouraged to come to the library to do research work. The State Library devotes its entire book fund to technical, professional and literary titles. The Law Section is particularly well equipped with material of importance to the law enforcement officer, and the other sections make a constant effort to acquire current titles along such lines.

C. **University Libraries.**

    1. The Library of the University of California at Berkeley consists of one main collection, three branch libraries, and 85 departmental and special libraries. These groups, collectively known as the University Library, contain more than a million volumes, plus approximately 16,000 periodicals and serials which are received currently.*

        a. The Bureau of Public Administration Library is located in Room 117 of the Main Library Building. It maintains an extensive collection of current pamphlets, periodicals, and documents relating to the work of government. Its index file is conceded to be the most complete file available in the field of administration of criminal justice in the United States.

        b. Through the Inter-library Loan Department the city and county libraries may borrow books from the University Library.

    2. Other universities have well-established libraries. While the collections are usually intended for the use of the students, in case of urgent need individual books could undoubtedly be borrowed or consulted.

---

* Comparable facilities are available in other states.

D. **Interlibrary Loan System.** The use of the interlibrary loan system in California has been mentioned in preceding paragraphs. It is interesting to note that in this state it has been developed to a most successful degree. Librarians everywhere are accustomed and willing to borrow from other libraries. The State Library maintains a Union Catalog which shows all the books available in the Library of Congress at Washington and in the county libraries and some of the city libraries of California. Thus it is possible to find the location of any desired book by asking the local librarian to secure the information, and if the book is available, to have the book borrowed in the same way.

II. LIBRARY ORGANIZATION

A. The head librarian is the trained manager in charge of the organization and over-all functions of the library. There are, of course, department heads and assistants who are trained to make accessible to the public all the resources of the library. You should learn how to use the library and its materials, but if any difficulties are encountered, you can always rely on the librarian to come to your aid.

B. The Book Stacks house the library's main book collection. They may be:

1. Open shelf—books are accessible to the public.

2. Closed shelf—books are not directly accessible to the public. They must be obtained through the facilities of the circulation department.

3. Reserved shelf—books which are in great demand, rare books, and certain books because of their subject content which are not immediately accessible to the public. These books must be obtained from the circulation department or the reserved bookroom. There are various restrictions limiting their general use and circulation.

    C. Order Department.

        1. In charge of the acquisition of books, periodicals, and other printed materials.

        2. This department also may attend to the binding or re-binding of the library's collection of printed materials.

    D. The catalog department.

        1. Classification of books.

        2. Preparation for the shelves.

        3. Makes the necessary call cards for the card catalog.

    E. The circulation department.

        1. Acts as custodian of the library's collection of books.

        2. Lends books to library members, keeping records as to what books are out, who has them, and when they are due to be returned.

        3. Has charge of reserved bookroom. Books in great demand are placed on reserve and are issued for a period of a few hours or overnight.

    F. The reference department.

        1. Helps users of the library to locate material, understand indexes, catalogs, encyclopedias, etc.

        2. Has charge of the reference tools and materials.

        3. May have charge of the periodical room.

    G. The Foregoing Elements are common to most libraries, although libraries do differ as to details of organization and purpose.

III. CLASSIFICATION OF BOOKS

In order to properly store books and locate them when needed, it has been necessary for libraries to use a classification system. Therefore, each book is assigned a call number consisting of two parts: the class, or subject number, which is placed above, and the author number, which appears below. Books are shelved according to subject and then alphabetically by author within the group. There are two systems of classification in general use: The

Dewey Decimal system and the Library of Congress Classification.

A.   The Dewey Decimal classification divides all of man's knowledge into 10 classes, and each of these 10 groups into 10 more groups, and so on for further subdivisions:

000 General Works	500 Science
100 Philosophy	600 Useful Arts
200 Religion	700 Fine Arts
300 Social Sciences	800 Literature
400 Philology	900 History

The Decimal classification is capable of almost indefinite expansion. A partial extension of the social science classification (300), is as follows:

     301 Philosophy, Theories
     302 Sociology for Teachers
     303 Encyclopedias
     304 Essays, addresses
     305 Yearbooks
340 Law
     341 International law and relations
     342 Constitutional law and history
     343 Capital punishment
     344 United States law, statutes, etc.
     345 Treatises on law
350 Administration
     351 Federal and State Government
     352 Municipal Government
     353 U. S. and State Government
     354 Military Science, Army
     359 Naval Science
360 Associations and Institutions
     361 Social Work
     362 Hospitals, Asylums
     363 Political Institutions
     364 Criminology, Juvenile Courts, Reformation
     365 Prisons

367 Clubs

368 Insurance

The following are some typical examples of call numbers for books in the field of law enforcement:

351.74 Perkins, Rollins M.

P. 419 *Elements of Police Science*

353.9 Smith, Bruce

Sm 5 *The State Police, Organization and Administration*

364 Soderman, Harry and O'Connell, John J.

So 16 *Modern Criminal Investigation*

The Library of Congress Classification uses the letters of the alphabet as its basis and adds to them arabic numerals. This system is employed by libraries with large collections, such as the University of California Library and the Library of Congress:

A General Works

B Philosophy

BF Psychology

BL–BX Religion

C Auxiliary. History

D History and Topography (except American)

D–F American

G Geography. Anthropology

H Social Sciences

J Political Science

K Law

L Education

M Music

N Fine Arts

OP Language and Literature

Q Science

R Medicine

S Agriculture. Plant and Animal Industry

T Technology

U Military Science

V Naval Science

Z Bibliography and Library Science

The Library of Congress Classification and the equivalent Dewey Decimal classification are listed below
for the purpose of comparison:

Library of Congress	Dewey Decimal	Book
HV 8073	364	*Modern Criminal Investi-*
SS 6	So 16	*gation* by Soderman & O'Connell
HV 7911	920	*Night Stock* by L. J. Val-
V 3A3	V 234	entine

IV. THE CARD CATALOG (Index to Materials)
The guide or index to the books in a library is the card
catalog. This is contained in a series of trays in some cen-
tral location. The catalog consists of a file of 3 × 5 cards
arranged alphabetically, containing information about the
individual books. In most libraries any book may be
found in the catalog in three ways: under the last name
of the author, under the title of the book, and under the
subject treated in the book. Cards may be also made for
translator, joint author, editor, compiler, etc.
A. The Author Card.

351.74
P 419   Perkins, Rollins Morris, 1889–
          Elements of Police Science, by Rollins M. Perkins . . . Chicago,
          The Foundation Press, Inc., 1942 xxii, 651 p. incl. front., illus.,
          forms 23¹/₂ cm. 1. Police 2. Criminal Law—U. S. I Title

---

In the upper left-hand corner is the classification or
call number. This is the number under which the
book is arranged on the library shelves to be located
by the borrower, or written down on a borrower's
card or "call slip" so that the librarian can locate it.
The first line gives the author's full name and his date
of birth. The second line describes the book by title,
author's name, place of publication, name of publisher and date of publication.
The next section (in small sized type) is called the
collation and indicates that there is a preface of 22
preliminary pages, 651 pages in the text proper, a

statement of illustrative material, and the size of the book in terms of centimeters.

The section below lists the subjects under which one can find catalog cards for this book. They are also useful in locating other printed material on the same or related subjects.

Cards carry numbers at the bottom which are of value and interest to librarians.

B. The Title Card.

```
351.74
P 419   Elements of Police Science
        Perkins, Rollins Morris, 1889–
        Elements of Police Science, by Rollins M. Perkins . . . Chicago, etc.
```

C. Subject Card.

```
351.74
P 419   Police
        Perkins, Rollins Morris, 1889–
        Elements of Police Science, etc.
```

A catalog card may also be found under the subject heading: Criminal Law—U. S.

D. Corporate Entry Cards.

Many books have no authors, but are issued under the name of the organization responsible for their production. The author is considered to be the organization (Carnegie Steel Corporation, California State Department of Education, etc.) itself rather than the compiler or material writer.

```
331.17
C 128 E   California, University, Bureau of Public Administration
          . . . . Estimate of California Employment and Unemployment.
          1946–1947 etc.
```

E. Subject Headings.

Frequently, persons looking for material on a particular subject do not know what has been written concerning the subject. Therefore, it is necessary that the card catalog subject headings be logical and uniform so that they can locate books through the catalog with a minimum expenditure of time and effort. An examination of the card catalog in any library will indicate under what subject heading it will be possible to locate material on a particular subject. Through the cross reference system of filing cards, it is possible to narrow the search down to one or two subject headings. Also, uniformity of subject entry in different libraries is achieved through the use of a published subject heading list, such as that issued by the American Library Association.

Since many subjects are broad and include many ramifications, it is necessary to modify the main subject heading by using sub-headings, arranged alphabetically or chronologically. Books on law enforcement and related fields may be located under the subject entry, "Crime and Criminals." This is a broad subject, however, and it is necessary to subdivide it to facilitate the location of books. For example:

Crime and Criminals
   General
   Identification
   Bibliography
   California
   California—Los Angeles
   California—San Francisco
   Chicago
   Denver
   England—London
   France
   Germany
   Great Britain
   New York—state
   New York—city
   United States
   Wyoming
   Etc.

F. Cross Reference.
  1. "See" cards refer the reader from the subject under which he looks to the headings under which printed material is entered in the card catalog.

State and Church

                              see

Church and State

Criminal Responsibilities

                              see

Crime and Criminals

---

  2. "See also" cards refer one from the heading under which he found some material to other related material.   Also, from general to specific headings.

Police Power

                          see also

Civil Rights; Constitutional Law; eminent domain; Government regulation of industry.

Crime and Criminals

                          see also

Adulterations; anarchism and anarchists; bribery; brigands and robbers; capital punishment; etc.

V. PERIODICAL INDEXES

Because periodicals are the most important source of up-to-the-minute information on a subject, the periodical indexes are indispensable in locating this information.   Each index lists articles appearing in a selected group of magazines.   The indexes appear monthly or at other regular intervals and are later cumulated into large bound volumes.   Periodical indexes are to be found in the reference room of a library.

  A. *Readers' Guide to Periodical Literature.*   (New York: The H. W. Wilson Co., 1900 to date.)
     Covers articles of a popular and general nature.   All articles are indexed under subject and author, and frequently under the title.   Published semi-monthly, and cumulated monthly, quarterly, annually, and biennially.

B. *Industrial Arts Index.* (New York: The H. W. Wilson Co., 1914 to date.)
Indexes over 235 periodicals on business, guidance, applied science and technology. Includes books, public documents and pamphlets. Author entries are omitted.

C. *International Index to Periodicals.* (New York: The H. W. Wilson Co., 1913 to date.)
Indexes over 250 American and foreign magazines containing articles on science and the humanities. Published bi-monthly and cumulated at intervals.

D. *Public Affairs Information Service.* (New York: P.A.I.S., 1915 to date.)
Valuable for books, magazines, pamphlets, government documents, mimeographed material in the fields of government and sociology. Subject entries only. Published weekly and cumulated five times a year.

E. *New York Times Index.* (New York: *New York Times,* 1913 to date.)
A valuable guide to all important articles appearing in this newspaper. Subject entries only. Published monthly and cumulated annually.

VI. DICTIONARIES.

A dictionary is a valuable reference book for all problems concerning words or phrases. The book is arranged alphabetically containing words, their meaning, spelling, pronunciation, derivation, and correct usage. There are many excellent dictionaries, but this pamphlet will list only a few of them.

A. *Webster's New International Dictionary of the English Language.*

B. Funk and Wagnalls *New Standard Dictionary.*

C. Crabb, George, *Crabb's English Synonyms.*

D. Allen, Frederic S., *English Synonyms and Antonyms.*

E. Mawson, C. O. S., *Roget's International Thesaurus of English Words and Phrases.*

VII. ENCYCLOPEDIAS

Standard encyclopedias, available in most libraries, are very helpful in providing concise information on any established subject, significant events, famous people and noted places. The articles are usually prepared by an accepted authority in a given field and are often supplemented by a list of books to which to turn for further information.

A. *Encyclopedia Britannica.* A new survey of international knowledge. (New York: Encyclopedia Britannica Co. c 1929.) A scholarly treatment of the subject matter. Index is in the last volume. Revised editions and supplements have been issued from time to time.

B. *Encyclopedia Americana.* (New York: Encyclopedia Americana Corp., 1918–20.)
A 30 volume scholarly set. Excellent for articles on business, government, science and technology. Various reissues supplemented by the Americana annual.

C. *Encylopedia of the Social Sciences.* (New York: Macmillan, 1930–35, 15 vols.)
Published under the auspices of ten American learned societies, this set is undoubtedly the most comprehensive and authoritative encyclopedia ever published in the field of social sciences.

D. *Social Work Year Book.* (New York: Russell Sage Foundation, 1930–date.)
A comprehensive work concerned with the problems of crime and criminality.

VIII. YEARBOOKS, ALMANACS AND MANUALS

These reference books contain significant facts and statistics on nearly every human activity. They are not directly concerned with the measuring of events or the interpretation of data. Only a few of these books are listed here.

A. *Stateman's Year Book.* (New York: The Macmillan Co., 1864–date.)
A statistical and historical annual of the states of the world. Contains statistics and facts concerning rules,

constitutions, governments, population, industries, etc. Has a bibliography for each country.

B. *The World Almanac.* (New York: World-Telegram. 1868–date.)
An extremely valuable collection of information, facts, and statistics on American finance, government, agriculture, trades, population, treaties, education, etc., in the last preceding year.

C. *Municipal Year Book.* (Chicago: International City Manager's Assn. 1934–date.)
An authoritative and comprehensive source for statistical data of American cities. Includes a directory of city officials and a selected list of books, pamphlets, and magazines.

IX. BIBLIOGRAPHY

A bibliography is a list of books and magazine articles on any given subject and is a most important source of information on that subject. Bibliographies vary widely in nature: some attempt to cover the subject completely, others are selective, and others cover only one phase of the subject. Some appear as books or pamphlets while others occupy only a few pages at the end of a volume. Since bibliographies appear in such different forms, it is advisable to consult the librarian when using such materials. Some of the bibliographies covering the field of law enforcement are:

A. Kuhlman, Augustus F.: *A Guide to Material on Crime and Criminal Justice.* . . .for the committee on survey of research on crime and criminal justice of the Social Science Research Council. (New York, 1929.) Limited to material published before January 1, 1927.

B. Culver, Dorothy Campbell: *Bibliography of Crime and Criminal Justice, 1927–1931.* (New York, 1939.)

C. Culver, Dorothy Campbell: *Bibliography of Crime and Criminal Justice, 1932–1937.* (New York, 1939.)

D. Greer, Sarah: *A Bibliography of Police Administration and Police Science.* (New York, Columbia University, 1936.)

E. Sellin, Thorsten and Shalle, J. P.: *A Bibliographical Manual for the Student of Criminology*. (Philadelphia, 1935.)

F. Cummings, John: *A Contribution Towards a Bibliography Dealing with Crime and Cognate Subjects*. (London, 1935.)

G. California State Department of Education. Bureau of Trade and Industrial Education. *A Suggested List of Reading of Interest to Policemen*. (Sacramento, 1936.)

H. International Association of Chiefs of Police. *A Selected Bibliography of Available Police Literature*.

I. Cabot, Phillipe S. de q.: *Juvenile Delinquency; a Critical Annotated Bibliography*. (New York, Wilson, 1946.) Contains 972 numbered entries of books and periodicals covering the period 1914–1944. Arranged alphabetically with subject entry.

X. LAW

There are many excellent indexes and references which may be employed in locating material on court decisions, laws, and magazine articles pertinent to the various fields of law enforcement. However, it is suggested that the county law librarian, regular public librarian, city attorney, or the district attorney be consulted if any difficulty is encountered in the search for material.

A. Verducci, Frances F., ed.: *Larmax Consolidated Index to Constitution and Laws of California*. (San Francisco, The Recorder Printing and Publishing Co., 1935-date.) A complete index under one alphabetical listing to the constitution, all 23 codes, the general laws and the rules of the supreme court, district court of appeals, superior and municipal courts. Suggestions of related topics by subject matters, filing systems, law and motion, probate days, and text of rules of court.

B. *Index to Legal Periodicals and Law Library Journal*. (New York, The H. W. Wilson Co., 1914-date.)

C. Coffey, Hobert: *Guide to Legal Materials.* (Ann Arbor, Overbeck, 1949.)

D. Doubles, M. R. and Farmer, F.: *Manual of Legal Bibliography.* (Charlottesville, The Michie Case Book Co., 1947.)

E. Dowling, N. T., Patterson, E. W., and Powell, R. R.: *Materials on Legal Methods.* (Chicago, Foundation Press, 1946.)

F. Ballentine, J. A. *Law Dictionary with Pronunciations.* (New York Cooperative Publishing Co., 1948.)

G. Black, Henry C. *Law Dictionary.* (St. Paul, West 1933.) Definitions of the terms and phrases of American and English jurisprudence, ancient and modern.

H. Bouvier, John. *Law Dictionary and Concise Encyclopedia.* (St. Paul, West, 1943.)

I. Fricke, C. W. *California Peace Officers' Manual.* (Los Angeles, O. W. Smith, 1949.) An outline of California Criminal law and procedure, explaining penal code sections, methods of investigation, rules of evidence, and law of arrest.

J. Fricke, C. W. *California Criminal Evidence.* (Los Angeles, Smith, 1945.) This book puts into concise and practical form the law of California laid down by statute and decision.

K. Fricke, C. W. *California Criminal Law.* (Los Angeles, Smith, 1949.) Explains Penal Code sections and gives the principles of criminal law applicable to all crimes, supported by leading and latest citations supplemented with illustrative cases.

L. Fricke, C. W.: *California Criminal Procedure.* (Los Angeles, Smith, 1949.)

M. *Deering's Civil Code of the State of California.* (San Francisco, Bancroft-Whitney, 1949.)

N. *Deering's Code of Civil Procedure of the State of California.* (San Francisco, Bancroft-Whitney, 1949.)

O. *Deering's General Laws of the State of California.* (San Francisco, Bancroft-Whitney, 1944, supplements issued.)

P. *Penal Code of the State of California.* Issued by various publishers such as: Bancroft-Whitney and O. W. Smith.

Q. Chase, Eugene J.: *California Codes.* (San Francisco, Chase Law Book Co., 1947.) Contains civil, probate, penal codes and codes of civil procedure.

R. *Standard Codes: Civil, Penal, Procedure, Probate.* (San Francisco, Bancroft-Whitney, 1935, supplements issued.)

S. McKinney, Wm. M., ed.: *California Jurisprudence.* (San Francisco, Bancroft-Whitney, 1935, supplements issued.)

T. McKinney, Wm. M., ed.: *New California Digest.* (San Francisco, Bancroft-Whitney, 1930, supplements issued.) Digest of all reported cases.

U. Witkins, B. E.: *Summary of California Law.* (San Francisco, The Author 1946.) A concise and critical manual of the Law of California.

V. *Reports of Cases Determined in the Supreme Court of the State of Calilfornia.* (San Francisco, Bancroft-Whitney, 1949.) Earlier editions issued.

W. *California Reports.* (San Francisco, Bancroft-Whitney.)

X. *California Appellate Reports.* (San Francisco, Bancroft-Whitney.)

Y. *Shepard's California Citations, Cases.* (New York, Shepard, 1946, supplement.)

Z. *Shepard's California Citations, Statutes.* (New York, Shepard, 1946, supplements.)

Note: The foregoing list is not exhaustive. It is strongly recommended that the peace officer consult his county or city Law Librarian, the District Attorney, or the California State Law Librarian regarding any of the above or additional references.

XI. FEDERAL BUREAU OF INVESTIGATION

    A. *The F. B. I. Law Enforcement Bulletin.* This is a monthly bulletin containing identification material. It also contains articles on some of the latest developments in criminal investigation. At regular intervals one of the issues will contain an index of all the material that has appeared in the bulletin since the last index was issued. Restricted to the use of law enforcement officials.

    B. *Uniform Crime Reports.* 1930-date. vol. nos. 1–7, 1930, published by the International Association of Chiefs of Police; V.1. no. 8, 1930-date, published by the U. S. Department of Justice, Federal Bureau of Investigation.

XII. MISCELLANEOUS INDEXES AND REFERENCES

There is an unlimited number of indexes and reference books covering practically every subject known to man. They have not been included here since they are not of immediate importance to the general field of police work. However, a few are included in this section simply to indicate what is actually available.

    A. Mudge, Isadore G. *Guide to Reference Books,* (Chicago, American Library Association, 1935, supplements.) The standard work for all questions connected with reference books and for information about them. An invaluable guide for those who need a guide to point out the reference tools available for some particular subject.

    B. *Who's Who in America,* a biographical dictionary of notable living men and women in the United States, 1899-date. Issued every two years. Contains concise biographical sketches of distinguished living Americans.

    C. *Book Review Digest.* (New York, The H. W. Wilson Co., 1905-date.) A digest and index of book reviews appearing in English and American periodicals. Each entry has a brief description note and excerpts from book reviews. Issued monthly and cumulated in annual volumes.

D. *Cumulative Books Index.* (New York, The H. W. Wilson Co., 1933-date.) A world list of books in the English language. Published monthly and cumulated at various intervals.

E. Bartlett, John.: *Familiar Quotations.* (Boston, Title, Brown and Co., 1914-date.) A collection of passages, phrases, and proverbs traced to their sources in ancient and modern literature. Revised editions are published from time to time.

F. *Biological Abstracts.* (Menasha, Wisconsin, Union of American Biological Societies. 1925-date.)
    A comprehensive abstracting and indexing journal of the world's literature in theoretical and applied biology.

G. *Chemical Abstracts.* (Easton Pennsylvania, American Chemical Society, 1907-date.)

Application

A. The instructor should bring to class sample catalog cards and several of the more useful and popular indexes and reference tools. The H. W. Wilson Company publishes sample pages from the Readers' Guide to Periodical Literature. If obtainable, they should be used in the classroom.

B. Select a topic related to police work and use in index to determine if any material has been published on the subject.

C. Discuss how to use an index and the meaning of abbreviations and symbols which are commonly used. For example: Sci Am 12:592–611 Ag '40 means, Scientific American, Volume 12, pages 592 through 611 in the August 1940 issue. Or it may be listed in a bibliography as: Scientific American 12 (Aug., 1940), 592–611.

Test

Practical test: Grade officers on their ability to locate and identify material on a particular subject. Use the Readers' Guide to periodical Literature. An objective type test should be given at the conclusion of the lessons contained in this section.

PART IV

BIBLIOGRAPHY

INTRODUCTION

This bibliography represents a carefully selected and comprehensive list of basic literature in the police field. It lists only those items which are considered to be practical, authentic, and reliable.

The bibliography is divided into two parts:

Part I *Bibliography Arranged According to the Occupational Analysis of the Police Service*

In this section the references are conveniently arranged according to the primary occupational blocks of the police service, i.e.:

Block number	*Block name*
I	ADMINISTRATION
II	PATROL
III	TRAFFIC
IV	INVESTIGATION
V	VICE
VI	CRIME PREVENTION
VII	RECORDS
VIII	IDENTIFICATION
IX	COMMUNICATIONS
X	JAIL—DETENTION— CUSTODIAL CARE

They are classified within each block according to the subject and then arranged alphabetically within each particular group.

Part II *Bibliography Arranged Alphabetically*

The references are arranged by author in alphabetical order.

Explanatory Note:

All titles of pamphlets marked with an asterisk (*) may be procured from the California State Department of Education, Bureau of Trade and Industrial Education, Peace Officers' Training, 721 Capitol Ave., Sacramento 14, California. Peace officers interested in obtaining this material should write for a copy of *Available Reference Material Price List.*

This material is developed by experienced peace officers and used for instructional purposes in the departmental schools, zone schools and institutes operated in connection with the California Peace Officers' Training Program, the Peace Officers' Association of the State of California, and the Sheriffs' Association of the State of California.

In accordance with the rules set down by the Training and Education Committee of the Peace Officers' Association of the State of California and the Sheriffs' Association of the State of California, this material is available only to regularly and full time employed peace officers as defined by the Penal Code of the State of California, State and Federal law enforcement agencies; with the following exceptions: *Law of Arrest; Criminal Law Outline; Criminal Law Course; Student Officers' Work Outline Emphasizing Elements of Major Crime; Rules of Evidence;* and *Basic Course in Firearms,* which are available to anyone.

A star (★) preceding a title indicates that the reference is recommended as a basic text for an officer's personal library.

BIBLIOGRAPHY

Arranged According To The
Occupational Analysis of the Police Service

I. **ORGANIZATION AND ADMINISTRATION**
   A. *General*
      SMITH, BRUCE: *Police Systems in the United States.* Rev. ed. New York: Harper, 1949. 351 pp.

VOLLMER, AUGUST: *The Police and Modern Society.* Berkeley: University of California Press, 1936. 253 pp.

Institute for Training in Municipal Administration. ★*Municipal Police Administration.* Rev. ed. Chicago, International City Managers' Association, 1950.

WILSON, O. W.: *Police Administration.* New York: McGraw-Hill Book Co., Inc., 1950. 540 pp.

LEONARD, V. A.: *Police Organization and Management.* The Foundation Press. Brooklyn: 1951. 507 pp.

PEPER, JOHN P., VOLLMER, AUGUST AND BOOLSEN, FRANK M.: *Police Organization and Administration.* California State Department of Education, Bureau of Industrial Education, Sacramento, 1951. 217 pp.

B. Law

BAKER, RUSSELL: *Manual on the Law of Arrest, Search and Seizure.* Chicago, Chicago Crime Commission, 1944. 49 pp.

California. Department of Education. Bureau of Trade and Industrial Education. *Civil Process and Procedure.* Sacramento, 1949. 16 pp.

——: ★*Criminal Law Outline.*★ Sacramento: 1949. 109 pp.

——: ★*Criminal Law Course, Student Officers' Work Outline Emphasizing Elements of Major Crime.*★ Sacramento, 1949. 109 pp.

——: *Extradition and Rendition.*★ Sacramento, 1949. 13 pp.

California. Department of Education. Bureau of Trade and Industrial Education. *Law of Arrest.*★ Sacramento, 1949. 21 pp.

——. *Rules of Evidence.*★ Sacramento, 1949. 21 pp.

California. State Board of Equalization. ★*California Alcoholic Beverage Control Act* and *Related Constitutional Provisions.* Sacramento, 1949. 114 pp.

——. ★*Rules and Regulations Issued in Pursuance of Section 22 of Article XX of the Constitution of California and Alcoholic Beverage Control Act.* Sacramento, 1950. 24 pp.

California. Youth Authority. ★*California Laws Relating to Youthful Offenders, Including the Youth Authority Act, the Juvenile Court Law.* Sacramento, 1947. 92 pp.

Council of State Governments. *The Handbook of Interstate Crime Control.* Rev. ed. Chicago, The Council, 1949. 91 pp.

DAVID, LEON T.: *The Tort Liability of Public Officers.* Chicago, Public Administration Service, 1940. 93 pp.

DAY, CARL E.: *Handbook of California Evidence.* San Francisco, The Author, 1948. 192 pp.

FRICKE, CHARLES W.: ★*California Criminal Evidence.* Los Angeles, O. W. Smith, 1945. 404 pp.

——. ★*California Criminal Law.* 3rd ed. Los Angeles: O. W. Smith, 1949. 470 pp.

——. ★*California Criminal Procedure.* 2nd rev. ed. Los Angeles, O. W. Smith, 1949. 470 pp.

——. ★*California Peace Officers' Manual.* Rev. 7th ed. Los Angeles, O. W. Smith, 1949. 259 pp.

——. *Digest of California Criminal Decisions, 1942–1947.* Los Angeles, Peace Officers Civil Service Ass'n., 1947. 205 pp.

LEWIS, ELMER A., comp.:   *Crime, Kidnapping and Prison Laws,*
Washington: Government Printing Office, 1941. 199 pp.

MASON, PAUL, comp.:   ★*Constitution of the State of California and of
the United States and Other Documents.* Sacramento, State Printing Office, 1949. 329 pp.

MICHAEL, JEROME AND HERBERT WECHSLER: *Criminal Law and its
Administration.* Chicago, Foundation Press, 1940. 1410 pp.

PUTTKAMMER, ERNST W.:   *Manual on Criminal Law Procedure.* Chicago, Chicago Crime Commission, 1946. 89 pp.

SULLIVAN, J. J.:   *Criminal Procedure in Municipal, Justice and City
Courts of California.* St. Paul, West, 1948. 498 pp.

TRISKA, JOSEPH F.:   ★*Juvenile Laws in California.* 2nd ed. Los
Angeles, 1948. 380 pp.

WAITE, JOHN B.:   *Criminal Law and Its Enforcement.* 3rd ed.
Brooklyn Foundation Press, 1947. 902 pp.

WIGMORE, JOHN H.:   ★*Code of the Rules of Evidence in Trials at
Law.* 3rd ed. Boston Little, Brown, 1942. 620 pp.

——. *Science of Judicial Proof.* 3rd ed. rev. Boston, Little, Brown,
1937. 1065 pp.

C. *Municipal Police Administration*

California. Department of Education. Bureau of Trade and Industrial Education. ★*Police Organization and Administration.** Sacramento, 1950.

COOPER, ROBERT W. *Municipal Police Administration in Texas.* Austin, University of Texas, 1938. 320 pp.

Institute for Training in Municipal Administration. ★*Municipal Police
Administration.* Rev. ed. Chicago, International City Managers'
Association, 1950.

D. *Personnel Management*

Chicago Crime Commission. *Police Standards.* Chicago, The Commission, 1942. 5 pp.

Civil Service Assembly. *Employee Relations in the Public Service.*
Chicago, The Assembly, 1942. 246 pp.

——. *Oral Tests in Public Personnel Selection.* Chicago, The Assembly,
1943. 164 pp.

——. *Placement and Probation in the Public Service.* Chicago, The
Assembly, 1946. 201 pp.

——. *Position-Classification in the Public Service.* Chicago, The
Assembly, 1941. 404 pp.

——. *Recruiting Applicants for the Public Service.* Chicago, The
Assembly, 1942. 200 pp.

HOLCOMB, RICHARD L.:   ★*Selection of Police Officers.* Iowa City,
State University of Iowa, Institute of Public Affairs, 1946. 94 pp.

HUBBARD, HENRY F.:   *The Elements of a Comprehensive Personnel
Program.* Chicago, Civil Service Assembly, 1947. 17 pp.

International City Managers' Association. ★*Municipal Personnel Administration.* Chicago, The Association, 1947. 435 pp.

LAIRD, DONALD A.:   *The Techniques of Personal Analysis.* New
York, McGraw-Hill, 1945. 408 pp.

MOSHER, WILLIAM E. AND J. DONALD KINGSLEY: ★*Public Personnel Administration.* New York, Harper, 1942. 671 pp.

Municipal Finance Officers Association. Committee on Public Employee Retirement Administration. *Retirement Plans for Public Employees.* Chicago, The Association, 1946. 36 pp.

PIGORS, PAUL AND CHARLES A. MEYERS: ★*Personnel Administration.* New York, McGraw-Hill, 1947. 553 pp.

PROBST, JOHN B.: *Measuring and Rating Employee Value.* New York, Ronald Press, 1947. 166 pp.

Public Administration Service. *Merit System Installation.* Chicago, Public Administration Service, 1941. 58 pp.

ROETHLISBERGER, FRITZ J.: ★*Management and Morale.* Cambridge: Harvard University Press, 1941. 194 pp.

——. WILLIAM J. DICKSON, AND HAROLD A. WRIGHT: *Management and the Worker.* Cambridge, Harvard University Press, 1939. 615 pp.

SCOTT, WALTER DILL, ROBERT C. CLOTHIER, AND WILLIAM R. SPRIEGEL: ★*Personnel Management.* 4th ed. New York, McGraw-Hill, 1949. 648 pp.

STONE, DONALD C. ★*Recruitment of Policemen.* Chicago, International Association of Chiefs of Police, 1938. 28 pp.

E. *Planning*

American Society of Planning Officials. *A Manual of Recommended Personnel Standards in Public Planning.* Chicago, The Society, 1949. 37 pp.

BLACK, RUSSEL VAN NEST: *Planning for the Small American City,* Rev. ed. Chicago, Public Administration Service, 1944. 86 pp.

OWSLEY, ROY H.: *City Plans for Promoting Industrial Peace.* Chicago, American Municipal Association, 1947. 32 pp.

WILSON, O. W.: *Police Planning.* Springfield, Illinois, Charles C Thomas Publisher, 1952. 500 pp.

F. *Public Administration*

GRAVES, WILLIAM B.: ★*Public Administration in a Democratic Society.* Boston, Health, 1950. 759 pp.

GULICK, LUTHER AND L. URWICK: ★*Papers on the Science of Administration.* New York, Columbia University, Institute of Public Administration, 1937. 195 pp.

International City Managers' Association. *The Technique of Municipal Administration.* Chicago, The Association, 1947. 601 pp.

PFFIFNER, JOHN: ★*Public Administration.* Rev. ed. New York, Ronald Press, 1946. 621 pp.

WHITE, LEONARD D.: ★*Introduction to the Study of Public Administration.* 3rd ed. New York, Macmillan, 1948. 612 pp.

G. *Public Relations*

California. Department of Education. Bureau of Trade and Industrial Education. *Public Relations.** Sacramento: 1949. 8 pp.

——. *Public Relations.** Sacramento, 1949. 11 pp.

——. *Public Speaking.** Sacramento, 1949. 8 pp.

International City Managers' Association, *Municipal Public Relations.* Chicago, The Association, 1940. 50 pp.

H. *Special Problems*

Detroit. Bureau of Governmental Research. *Police Precincts: How Many Precincts are Necessary for Efficient and Economical Operations of the Police Department.* Report No. 159. Detroit, 1945. 17 pp.

International Association of Chiefs of Police. ★*Police Unions and Other Police Organizations.* Washington, The Association, 1944. 30 pp.

MAGNUSSON, LEIFUR: *Government and Union-Employer Relations: An Analysis of Statutes and Administrative Regulations.* Chicago, Public Administration Service, 1945. 36 pp.

Municipal Finance Officers' Association. *Accounting for Government-Owned Motor Equipment.* Chicago, The Association, 1940. 60 pp.

——. *Accounting for Governmental Supplies.* Chicago, The Association, 1940. 60 pp.

——. *Municipal Budget Procedure and Budgetary Accounting.* Chicago, The Association, 1942. 100 pp.

Peace Officers' Association of the State of California. *The Crime Prevention Committee's Report on Subversive Activities.* (1940). 19 pp.

PFFIFNER, JOHN: ★*A Manual for Administrative Analysts.* Los Angeles, University of Southern California, 1947.

Public Administration Service. *Work Simplification: As Exemplified by the Work Simplification Program of the U. S. Bureau of the Budget.* Chicago, Public Administration Service, 1945. 49 pp.

WILLIAMS, CAROL M.: *Organization and Practices of Policewomen Divisions in the United States.* Detroit, National Training School of Public Service, 1946. 40 pp.

WILSON, O. W.: *Distribution of Police Patrol.* Chicago: Public Administration Service, 1941. 27 pp.

I. *State and Rural Police*

California. Department of Education. Bureau of Trade and Industrial Education. ★*Powers and Duties of the Sheriff and Other County Offices.*★ Sacramento, 1949. 13 pp.

MONROE, DAVID G.: *State and Provincial Police; a Study in Police Functioning in the United States and Canada.* Chicago, International Association of Chiefs of Police, 1941. 251 pp.

SMITH, BRUCE: *Rural Crime Control.* New York, Institute of Public Administration, 1933. 306 pp.

——. *State Police.* New York, Macmillan, 1925. 281 pp.

VOLLMER, AUGUST, AND ALFRED E. PARKER. *Crime and the State Police.* Berkeley: University of California Press, 1935. 226 pp.

J. *Supervision and Leadership*

BECKMAN, R. O.: ★*How to Train Supervisors.* 3rd rev. ed. New York, Harper, 1948. 329 pp.

BROADED, C. H.: ★*Essentials of Management for Supervisors.* New York, Harpers, 1947. 239 pp.

CUSHMAN, FRANK, AND ROBERT W. CUSHMAN: *Improving Supervision.* New York, Wiley, 1947. 232 pp.

GOCKE, B. W.: ★*Police Sergeants Manual.* Los Angeles, O. W. Smith, 1946. 312 pp.

HALSY, GEORGE D.: *Supervising People.* New York, Harper, 1946. 233 pp.

HOLDEN, PAUL E., LOUNSBURY S. FISH, AND HUBERT L. SMITH: ★*Top-Management Organization and Control.* Stanford, University of Stanford Press, 1941. 239 pp.

LAIRD, DONALD A.: *The Techniques of Handling People.* New York, McGraw-Hill, 1947. 138 pp.

PFFIFNER, JOHN: ★*Supervision of Personnel.* Los Angeles, University of Southern California. 1949.

SCHELL, ERWIN H.: *The Technique of Executive Control.* 6th ed. New York, McGraw-Hill, 1946. 270 pp.

SPRIEGEL, WILLIAM R., AND EDWARD SCHULZ. ★*Elements of Supervision.* New York, Wiley, 1942. 273 pp.

TEAD, ORDWAY: *Art of Leadership.* New York, McGraw-Hill, 1935. 308 pp.

K. *Training*

California. Department of Education. Bureau of Trade and Industrial Education. ★*A Study Manual and Bibliography for Peace Officers.** Sacramento, 1950.

——. *Conference Leader Training.* Sacramento, 1943. 39 pp.

Civil Service Assembly. *Employee Training in the Public Service.* Chicago, The Assembly, 1941. 172 pp.

CUSHMAN, FRANK: ★*Training Procedure.* New York, Wiley, 1940. 230 pp.

FRICKE, CHARLES W.: *1000 Police Questions and Answers for the California Peace Officer.* 4th ed. Los Angeles, O. W. Smith, 1946. 75 pp.

——. *5000 Criminal Definitions, Terms and Phrases.* 2nd ed. Los Angeles, O. W. Smith, 1949. 121 pp.

JACKEY, DAVID F., AND MELVIN L. BARLOW: ★*The Craftsman Prepares to Teach.* New York, Macmillan, 1944. 184 pp.

LEVIN, FRANK K.: ★*How to Read for Self-Improvement.* Chicago, American Technical Society, 1947. 246 pp.

NEWTON, ROY. *How to Improve Your Personality.* New York, McGraw-Hill, 1949. 205 pp.

PERKINS, ROLLIN M.: ★*Police Examinations.* Brooklyn, Foundation Press, 1947. 431 pp.

TAYLOR, CLARENCE P.: ★*A Traffic Officer's Training Manual.* Chicago, National Safety Council, 1930. 225 pp.

II. PATROL

A. *Basic Methods and Procedures*

ADAMS, FRANK H.: ★*Basic Criminal Psychiatry with Emphasis on Sex Crimes.** Sacramento, Department of Education, Peace Officers' Training, 1950.

California. Department of Education. Bureau of Trade and Industrial Education. *Covering Roads for Wanted Cars and Fugitives.** Sacramento, 1949. 5 pp.

———. ★*Elements of Police Investigation.** Sacramento, 1950. 81 pp.

———. ★*Field Note Taking.** Sacramento, 1950. 31 pp.

———. ★*Patrol Procedure and Observation.** Sacramento, 1949. 20 pp.

———. ★*Transportation of Prisoners.** Sacramento, 1949. 4 pp.

CAHALANE, CORNELIUS F.: ★*Police Practices and Procedure.* New York, Dutton, 1914. 241 pp.

———. *The Policeman.* New York, Dutton, 1923. 354 pp.

CALLAN, GEORGE D., AND RICHARD STEPHENSON: *Police Methods for Today and Tomorrow.* Newark, Duncan Press, 1939. 361 pp.

HOLCOMB, RICHARD L.: *Police Patrol.* Springfield, Illinois, Charles C Thomas Publisher, 1952. 115 pp.

HUTZEL, ELEANOR L.: *Policewoman's Handbook.* New York, Columbia University Press, 1933. 303 pp.

MILES, ARNOLD: *How Criminals are Caught.* New York, Macmillan, 1939. 123 pp.

PERKINS, ROLLIN M.: ★*Elements of Police Science.* Chicago, Foundation Press, 1942. 615 pp.

ROBINTON, WALTER H.: *Basic Procedure in Law Enforcement.* Gainesville, University of Florida, 1943. 140 pp.

SKEHAN, JAMES J.: ★*Modern Police Work Including Detective Duty.* Rev. ed. New York, Basuino, 1948. 657 pp.

B. *First Aid*

American Red Cross. *First Aid Text-Book.* Rev. ed. Philadelphia, Blakiston, 1940. 256 pp.

JARVIS, FRED J.: First Aid, *in* Rollin M. Perkins, *Elements of Police Science.* Chicago, Foundation Press, 1942. pp. 181–193.

C. *Public Relations*

ADLOW, ELIJAH: ★*Policemen and the Public.* Boston, Rochfort, 1947. 89 pp.

California. Department of Education. Bureau of Trade and Industrial Education. *Court Appearance and Testimony.** Sacramento, 1949. 11 pp.

HOLCOMB, RICHARD L.: *The Police and the Public.* Iowa City, State University of Iowa, Institute of Public Affairs, 1950. 36 pp.

LADD, MASON: ★On the Witness Stand, *in* Rollin M. Perkins, *Elements of Police Science.* Chicago, Foundation Press, 1942. pp. 91–109.

OLANDER, OSCAR G.: Police Courtesy, *in* Rollin M. Perkins, *Elements of Police Science.* Chicago, Foundation Press, 1942. pp. 73–90.

D. *Riots and Disorders*

California. Department of Justice. ★*A Guide to Race Relations for Peace Officers,* by Davis McEntire and Robert E. Powers. Sacramento, 1946. 38 pp.

Chicago. Park District. *The Police and Minority Groups: A Manual Prepared for Use in the Chicago Park District Police Training School.* by Joseph D. Lohman. Chicago, 1947. 133 pp.

LEE, ALFRED McCLUNG, AND NORMAN DAYMOND HUMPHREY: *Race Riot.* New York, Dryden Press, 1943. 143 pp.

WOOD, STERLING A.: *Riot Control.* Harrisburg, Military Service Publishing Co., 1946. 155 pp.

E. *Self-Defense*

ALLEN, EDWARD L.: *American Jiu-Jitsu.* Toronto, Blue Ribbon, 1942.

ASKINS, CHARLES: *The Art of Handgun Shooting.* New York, Barnes, 1941. 219 pp.

BUTLER, J. F. Revolver Shooting, *in* Rollin M. Perkins, *Elements of Police Science.* Chicago, Foundation Press, 1942. pp. 194–219.

California. Department of Education. Bureau of Trade and Industrial Education. *Basic Course in Firearms.** Sacramento, 1949. 25 pp.

——. *Self Defense.** Sacramento: 1949. 15 pp.

KUWASHIMA, T. S.: *Judo; Forty-One Lessions in the Modern Science of Jiu-Jitsu.* New York, Putnam, 1949. 156 pp.

MATSUYAMA, FRANK: *Yawara Manual.* Denver, The Author, 1948. 78 pp.

ROPER, WALTER: *Pistol and Revolver Shooting.* New York, Macmillan, 1945. 256 pp.

III. **TRAFFIC**

A. *Accidents*

California. Department of Education. Bureau of Trade and Industrial Education. ★*Traffic Accident Investigation.** Sacramento, 1949. 23 pp.

——. *Traffic Accident Records and Analysis.** Sacramento, 1949. 14 pp.

HALSEY, MAXWELL N.: *Traffic Accidents and Congestion.* New York, Wiley, 1947. 408 pp.

Northwestern University Traffic Institute. ★*Accident Investigation Manual.* Rev. ed. Evanston, The Institute, 1948. 241 pp.

U. S. Federal Bureau of Investigation. *Traffic Control and Accident Investigation.* Chapel Hill, University of North Carolina, Institute of Government, 1947. 197 pp.

B. *Courts*

California. Department of Education. Bureau of Trade and Industrial Education. *Court Appearance and Testimony.** Sacramento, 1949. 11 pp.

FISHER, EDWARD: ★*People's Court.* Evanston, Northwestern University Traffic Institute, 1947. 164 pp.

WARREN, GEORGE: ★*Traffic Court.* New York, Little, Brown, 1942. 380 pp.

LADD, MASON: ★On the Witness Stand, *in* Rollin M. Perkins, *Elements of Police Science.* Chicago, Foundation Press, 1942. pp. 91–109.

C. *Drunk Driver Testing*

California. Department of Education. Bureau of Trade and Industrial Education. ★*Drunk Driver Testing—Use of Chemical Tests for Intoxication.** Sacramento, 1949. 53 pp.

DONIGAN, ROBERT L.: *Chemical Test Case Law.* Evanston, Northwestern University Traffic Institute, 1950. 83 pp.

FORRESTER, GLENN C.: *The Use of Chemical Tests for Alcohol in Traffic Law Enforcement.* Springfield, Illinois, Charles C Thomas, Publisher, 1949. 250 pp.

D. Enforcement

California. Department of Education. Bureau of Trade and Industrial Education. *Traffic (Selective) Enforcement.* Sacramento, 1949. 6 pp.

International Association of Chiefs of Police. ★*State Traffic Law Enforcement.* Chicago, The Association, 1944. 300 pp.

E. Engineering

California. Department of Education. Bureau of Trade and Industrial Education. *Traffic Engineering (Outline).* Sacramento, 1949. 9 pp.

EVANS, HENRY K., AND F. M. KREML: ★*Traffic Engineering and the Police.* Rev. ed. Evanston: International Association of Chiefs of Police and National Conservation Bureau, 1946. 103 pp.

HAMMOND, HAROLD F.: ★*Traffic Engineering Handbook.* New York, Institute of Traffic Engineers, National Conservation Bureau, 1941. 320 pp.

HAMMOND, H. F., AND F. M. KREML: *Traffic Engineering and the Police.* Evanston, Northwestern Traffic Institute, 1938. 285 pp.

F. Parking

SIO, ARNOLD A.: Parking—*What Cities are Doing.* Chicago, American Municipal Association, 1949, 17 pp.

G. Safety

BENNETT, RICHARD O.: *The Bicycle and Traffic Safety.* Evanston, Northwestern University Traffic Safety Institute, (1937). 75 pp.

California. Governor. Coordinating Committee of State Officials on Traffic Safety. *Plan of Action for Traffic Safety in California.* Sacramento, 1949. 22 pp.

Council of State Governments. *Highway Safety—Motor Truck Regulation.* Chicago, The Council, 1950. 198 pp.

IV. INVESTIGATION

A. Courts

California. Department of Education. Bureau of Trade and Industrial Education. *Court Appearance and Testimony.* Sacramento, 1949. 11 pp.

LADD, MASON: ★On the Witness Stand, *in* Rollin M. Perkins, *Elements of Police Science.* Chicago, Foundation Press, 1942. pp. 91–109.

B. Basic Methods and Procedures

MILES, ARNOLD: *How Criminals are Caught.* New York, Macmillan, 1939. 123 pp.

PERKINS, ROLLIN M.: ★*Elements of Police Science.* Chicago, Foundation Press, 1942. 615 pp.

ROBINTON, WALTER H.: *Basic Procedure in Law Enforcement.* Gainesville, University of Florida, 1943. 140 pp.

SKEHAN, JAMES J.: ★*Modern Police Work Including Detective Duty.* Rev. ed. New York, Basuino, 1948. 657 pp.

C. Criminal

ADAMS, FRANK H.: ★*Basic Criminal Psychiatry with Emphasis on Sex Crimes.* Sacramento, Department of Education, Peace Officers' Training, 1950.

California. Department of Education. Bureau of Trade and Industrial Education. ★*Laboratory Techniques in Criminal Investigation.*° Sacramento, 1949. 25 pp.

DIENSTEIN, WILLIAM: *Technics For the Crime Investigator.* Springfield, Illinois, Charles C Thomas, Publisher; 1952. 222 pp.

EISEMAN, JAMES S.: *Elements of Investigative Techniques.* Bloomington, McNight and McNight, 1949. 182 pp.

FRICKE, CHARLES W.: ★*Criminal Investigation.* Popular ed. Los Angeles, O. W. Smith, 1949. 79 pp.

GROSS, HANS: ★*Criminal Investigation.* London, Sweet and Maxwell, 1938. 558 pp.

SODERMAN, HARRY, AND JOHN J. O'CONNELL: ★*Modern Criminal Investigations.* Rev. ed. New York, Funk and Wagnalls, 1945. 478 pp.

U. S. War Department. ★*Criminal Investigation.* Field Manual FM 19–20. Washington: Government Printing Office, 1946. 358 pp.

VOLLMER, AUGUST: Criminal Investigation, *in* Rollin M. Perkins, *Elements of Police Science.* Chicago, Foundation Press, 1942. pp. 37–59.

D. Evidence

California. Department of Education. Bureau of Trade and Industrial Education. *Collection and Preservation of Evidence.*° Sacramento: 1949.

KREML, FRANK M.: ★*Evidence Handbook for Police.* Evanston, Northwestern University Traffic Institute, 1948. 150 pp.

E. Information

California. Department of Education. Bureau of Trade and Industrial Education. ★*Sources of Information.*° Sacramento, 1949. 29 pp.

F. Interrogation

BINGHAM, WALTER VAN DYKE, AND BRUCE VICTOR MOORE: *How to Interview.* 3rd Rev. ed. New York, Harper, 1941. 263 pp.

California. Department of Education. Bureau of Trade and Industrial Education. ★*Elements of Interrogation.*° Sacramento, 1949. 79 pp.

FISHER, JACOB: *The Art of Detection.* New Brunswick, Rutgers University Press, 1947. 248 pp.

INBAU, FRED E.: ★*Lie Detection and Criminal Interrogation.* 2nd Rev. ed. Baltimore, Williams and Wilkins, 1948. 193 pp.

LEE, CLARENCE D.: *The Instrumental Detection of Deception.* Springfield, Illinois, Charles C Thomas, Publisher, 1952.

LARSON, JOHN: *Lying and Its Detection.* Chicago, University of Chicago Press, 1932. 453 pp.

WELLMAN, F. L.: *The Art of Cross-Examination.* 4th ed. rev. New York, Macmillan, 1944. 479 pp.

G. Photography

Eastman Kodak Company. ★*Photography in Law Enforcement.* Rochester, The Company, 1948. 112 pp.

——. ★*How to Make Good Pictures.* 28th ed. Rochester, The Company, 1949. 240 pp.

HERZOG, A. S., AND A. J. EZICKSON: *Camera Take the Stand.* New York, Prentice-Hall, 1940. 195 pp.

KENT, FREDERICK W.: Photography, *in* Rollin M. Perkins, *Elements of Police Science.* Chicago, Foundation Press, 1942. pp. 117–143.

H. Riots and Disorders

California. Department of Justice. ★*A Guide to Race Relations For Peace Officers,* by Davis McEntire and Robert E. Powers. Sacramento, 1946. 38 pp.

Chicago. Park District. *The Police and Minority Groups; A Manual Prepared for Use in the Chicago Park District Police Training School,* by Joseph D. Lohman. Chicago, 1947. 133 pp.

LEE, ALFRED McCLUNG, AND NORMAN DAYMOND HUMPHREY. *Race Riot.* New York, Dryden Press, 1943. 143 pp.

WOOD, STERLING A.: *Riot Control.* Harrisburg, Military Service Publishing Co., 1946. 155 pp.

I. Specific Offenses

BOOS, WILLIAM F.: *The Poison Trail.* Boston, Cushman and Flint, 1939. 380 pp.

California. Department of Education. Bureau of Trade and Industrial Education. *Arson Investigation.*° Sacramento, 1949. 16 pp.

——. *Investigation of Auto Theft with Particular Reference to Modus Operandi.*° Sacramento, 1949. 26 pp.

California. Department of Education. Bureau of Trade and Industrial Education. *Bunco.*° Sacramento, 1949. 12 pp.

——. *Burglary-Residence.*° Sacramento, 1949. 7 pp.

——. *Burglary-Safes.*° Sacramento, 1949. 10 pp.

——. *Burglary-Commercial.*° Sacramento, 1949. 6 pp.

——. *Corporate Security Frauds.*° Sacramento, 1949. 6 pp.

——. *Investigation of Fictitious Checks.*° Sacramento, 1949. 6 pp.

——. *Grand Theft—Person.*° Sacramento, 1949. 7 pp.

——. *Investigation of Homicide.*° Sacramento, 1949. 23 pp.

——. *Robbery.*° Sacramento, 1949. 4 pp.

——. *Investigation of Sex Crimes.*° Sacramento, 1949. 20 pp.

California. Highway Patrol. Division of Technical Services. *Auto Theft Investigation.* Sacramento, 1950. 36 pp.

California. Legislature. Interim Committee on Judicial System and Judicial Process. ★*Preliminary Report of the Subcommittee on Sex Crimes.* Sacramento, 1949. 269 pp.

KINSEY, A. C., W. B. POMEROY, AND C. E. MARTIN: ★*Sexual Behaviour in the Human Male.* New York, Saunders, 1948. 804 pp.

KRAFFT-EBING, RICHARD VON: ★*Psychopathia Sexualis.* London, Rebman, 1901. 585 pp.

McDONALD, JOHN C. ★*Crime is a Business.* Stanford, Stanford University Press, 1939. 363 pp.

RIVER, PAUL J. DE: *The Sexual Criminal.* Springfield, Illinois, Charles C Thomas, Publisher, 1949. 250 pp.

SNYDER, LeMOYNE. ★*Homicide Investigation.* Springfield, Illinois, Charles C Thomas, Publisher, 1949. 302 pp.

U. S. Federal Bureau of Investigation. ★*Some Technical Observations in the Detection of Sabotage.* Washington, 1942. 44 pp.

WILSON, FRANK J.: "Detection of Counterfeit Money", *in* Rollin M. Perkins, *Elements of Police Science*. Chicago, Foundation Press, 1942. pp. 61–72.

J. Surveillance

California. Department of Education. Bureau of Trade and Industrial Education. *Surveillance.** Sacramento, 1949. 35 pp.

V. VICE

A. Gambling

American Academy of Political and Social Science. Gambling, *The Annals*. 269 (May, 1950), 1–149.

B. Narcotics

California. Department of Education. Bureau of Trade and Industrial Education. *Narcotic Investigation and Narcotic Enforcement.** Sacramento, 1949. 19 pp.

California. Department of Justice. Division of Narcotic Enforcement. *Narcotic Act*. Sacramento, 1949. 29 pp.

HESSE, ERICH: *Narcotics and Drug Addiction*. Tr. by Frank Gaynor. New York, Philosophical Library, 1946. 219 pp.

LINDESMITH, ALFRED: *Opiate Addiction*. Bloomington, Principia Press, 1947. 238 pp.

WALTON, ROBERT P.: *Marihuana, America's New Drug Problem*. Philadelphia, Lippincott, 1938. 223 pp.

C. Prostitution

California. Department of Education. Bureau of Trade and Industrial Education. *Investigation of Prostitution.** Sacramento, 1949. 11 pp.

U. S. Federal Security Agency. *Techniques of Law Enforcement Against Prostitution*. Washington, Government Printing Office, 1943. 75 pp.

VI. CRIME PREVENTION

A. Criminology

BARNES, HARRY E., AND NEGLEY K. TEETERS: *New Horizons in Criminology; the American Crime Problem*. New York, Prentice-Hall, 1946. 1069 pp.

BRANHAM, VERNON C., AND SAMUEL B. KUTASH, eds.: *Encyclopedia of Criminology*. New York, Philosophical Library, 1949. 527 pp.

CAVAN, RUTH S.: *Criminology*. New York, Corwell, 1948. 762 pp.

HENTIG, HANS VON: *Crime; Causes and Condition*. New York, McGraw-Hill, 1947. 379 pp.

POLLAK, OTTO: *Criminality of Women*. Philadelphia, University of Pennsylvania Press, 1950. 180 pp.

RECKLESS, WALTER C.: *The Crime Problem*. New York, Appleton-Century-Crofts, 1950. 537 pp.

SUTHERLAND, EDWIN H.: *Principles of Criminology*. 4th ed. Chicago, Lippincott, 1947. 634 pp.

TAFT, DONALD R.: *Criminology*. New York, Macmillan, 1942. 708 pp.

VOLLMER, AUGUST: ★*The Criminal*. Brooklyn, Foundation Press, 1949. 462 pp.

B. *Juvenile Delinquency*

American Academy of Political and Social Science. Juvenile Delinquency, The Annals. 261 (Jan., 1949), 1–178.

California. Department of Education. Bureau of Trade and Industrial Education. *Juvenile Delinquency Control.** Sacramento, 1949. 33 pp.

——. *Juvenile Procedure.** Sacramento, 1949. 10 pp.

California. Department of Justice. ★Peace Officers *Manual on Juvenile Control.* Sacramento, 1944. 44 pp.

California. Youth Authority. Division of Delinquency Prevention. ★*An Outline of a Community Program for the Prevention of Juvenile Delinquency.* Sacramento, 1943. 12 pp.

ELLINGSTON, JOHN R.: *Protecting Our Children from Criminal Careers.* New York, Prentice-Hall, 1948. 374 pp.

MERRILL, MAUD: *Problems of Child Delinquency.* New York, Houghton-Mifflin, 1947. 403 pp.

PIGEON, HELEN D., and others: *Principles and Methods in Dealing with Offenders.* State College, Pa., Pennsylvania Municipal Publications Service, 1948. 442 pp.

Southern California. University. Delinquency Control Institute. ★*Administrative Aspects of Delinquency Control.* Los Angeles, University of Southern California, 1946. 74 pp.

Southern California. University. Delinquency Control Institute. ★*Delinquency Prevention Techniques.* Los Angeles, University of Southern California, 1947. 93 pp.

——. ★*Social Treatment Aspects of Delinquency Control.* Los Angeles, University of Southern California, 1946. 80 pp.

U. S. Federal Security Agency. Children's Bureau. ★*Techniques of Law Enforcement in the Treatment of Juveniles and the Prevention of Juvenile Delinquency.* Washington, Government Printing Office, 1944. 60 pp.

U. S. Federal Security Agency. Children's Bureau. ★*Understanding Juvenile Delinquency.* Washington, Government Printing Office, 1943. 52 pp.

C. *Psychology and Psychiatry*

ABRAHAMSEN, DAVID: *Crime and the Human Mind.* New York, Columbia University Press, 1944. 244 pp.

ADAMS, FRANK H.: ★*Basic Criminal Psychiatry with Emphasis on Sex Crimes.** Sacramento, Department of Education, Peace Officers' Training, 1950.

BROMBERG, WALTER: *Crime and the Mind; An Outline of Psychiatric Criminology.* Philadelphia, Lippincott, 1948. 219 pp.

DAWSON, WILLIAM S.: ★*Aids to Psychiatry.* 5th ed. Baltimore, Williams and Wilkins, 1944. 306 pp.

HUNT, J. MCVICKER, ed.: *Personality and Behavior Disorders.* New York, Ronald Press, 1944. 2 vols.

LINDNER, ROBERT M.: ★*Stone Walls and Men.* New York, Odyssey Press, 1946. 496 pp.

THORPE, LOUIS P., AND BARNEY KATZ: *The Psychology of Abnormal Behavior.* New York, Ronald Press, 1948. 877 pp.

WERTHAM, FREDERIC: *Show of Violence.* New York, Doubleday, 1949. 279 pp.

D. Youth Authority
California. *Youth Authority.* ★The Youth Authority, Organization and Program. Sacramento, 1945. 24 pp.

VII. RECORDS

A. Modus Operandi
ATCHERLY, LLEWLYN W., AND F. BROOK: *Modus Operandi.* London, His Majesty's Stationery Office, 1932. 90 pp.

California. Department of Justice. Division of Criminal Identification and Investigation. ★*Modus Operandi and Crime Reporting.* Sacramento, 1947. 17 pp.

California. Department of Education. Bureau of Trade and Industrial Education. ★*Modus Operandi Report Writing.* Sacramento, 1949. 22 pp.

B. Photographs
McDONALD, HUGH C., AND HARRY W. ROGER: *The Classification of Police Photographs.* Los Angeles, De Vorss, 1941. 89 pp.

C. Records
BROOKS, PHILIP C.: *Public Records Management.* Chicago, Public Administration Service. 1949. 19 pp.

California. Department of Education. Bureau of Trade and Industrial Education. *Traffic Accident Records and Analysis.** Sacramento, 1949. 14 pp.

——. *Police Records.** Sacramento, 1949. 9 pp.

——. *Use of Records.** Sacramento, 1949. 28 pp.

ODELL, MARGARET K., AND EARL P. STRONG: *Records Management and Filing Operations.* New York, McGraw-Hill, 1947. 342 pp.

WILSON, O. W.: ★*Police Records: Their Installation and Use.* 2nd ed. Chicago, Public Administration Service, 1948. 336 pp.

D. Reports and Report Writing
AURNER, ROBERT R.: *Effective Business English.* 3rd ed. Cincinatti, South-Western, 1949. 582 pp.

California. Department of Education. Bureau of Trade and Industrial Education. ★*Report Writing.** Sacramento, 1949. 12 pp.

International City Managers' Association. *Monthly Administrative Reports for Cities.* Chicago, The Association, 1949. 32 pp.

International City Managers' Association. *Specifications for the Annual Municipal Report.* Chicago, The Association, 1948. 52 pp.

International Association of Chiefs of Police. Committee on Uniform Crime Records. ★*Uniform Crime Reporting. A Complete Manual for Police.* Rev. ed. New York, The Association, 1949. 464 pp.

U. S. Federal Bureau of Investigation. ★*A Handbook Containing Suggestions for the Preparation of Uniform Crime Reports.* Washington, 1938. 91 pp.

——. ★*How to Use the Uniform Crime Reports.* Washington, 1939. 28 pp.

——. ★*Uniform Crime Reporting Handbook; Suggestions on Uniform Crime Reports.* Washington, 1943. 33 pp.

VIII. IDENTIFICATION

  A. *Criminal*

California. Department of Education. Bureau of Trade and Industrial Education. ★*Laboratory Techniques in Criminal Investigation.*° Sacramento, 1949. 25 pp.

——. ★*Collection and Preservation of Evidence.*° Sacramento, 1949. 22 pp.

CASTELLANOS, I.: *Identification Problems, Criminal and Civil.* New York, Basuino, 1939. 215 pp.

FRICKE, CHARLES W.: ★*Criminal Investigation.* Popular ed. Los Angeles, O. W. Smith, 1949. 79 pp.

GROSS, HANS: ★*Criminal Investigation.* London, Sweet and Maxwell, 1938. 586 pp.

KREML, FRANK M.: ★*Evidence Handbook for Police.* Evanston, Northwestern University Traffic Institute, 1948. 150 pp.

LUCAS, ALFRED: *Forensic Chemistry and Scientific Crime Investigation.* 4th ed. New York, Longmans, 1946. 340 pp.

O'HARA, CHARLES E., AND JAMES W. OSTERBURG: ★*An Introduction to Criminalistics.* New York, Macmillan, 1949. 705 pp.

PERKINS, ROLLIN M.: ★*Elements of Police Science.* Chicago, Foundation Press, 1942. 615 pp.

SODERMAN, HARRY, AND JOHN J. O'CONNELL: *Modern Criminal Investigation.* Rev. ed. New York, Funk and Wagnalls, 1945. 478 pp.

TURNER, RALPH F.: ★*Forensic Science and Laboratory Techniques.* Springfield, Illinois, Charles C Thomas, Publisher, 1949. 242 pp.

U. S. War Department. ★*Criminal Investigation.* Field Manual FM 19-20. Washington, Government Printing Office, 1946. 358 pp.

  B. *Court Appearance*

California. Department of Education. Bureau of Trade and Industrial Education. *Court Appearance and Testimony.*° Sacramento, 1949. 11 pp.

LADD, MASON: On the Witness Stand, *in* Rollin M. Perkins, *Elements of Police Science.* Chicago, Foundation Press, 1942. pp. 91–109.

  C. *Fingerprinting*

BATTLEY, HARRY: *Single Fingerprints.* New Haven, Yale University Press, 1931. 98 pp.

BRIDGES, B. C.: *Practical Fingerprinting.* New York, Funk and Wagnalls, 1942. 374 pp.

California. Department of Education. Bureau of Trade and Industrial Education. *Fingerprint Identification and Classification.*° Sacramento, 1949. 13 pp.

GESSELL, HAROLD J. E. Fingerprints, *in* Rollin M. Perkins, *Elements of Police Science.* Chicago, Foundation Press, 1942. pp. 144–180.

U. S. Federal Bureau of Investigation. ★*Classification of Fingerprints.* Washington, Government Printing Office.

  D. *Firearms*

HATCHER, JULIAN S.: *Notebook; a Standard Reference Book for Shooters, Gunsmiths, Ballisticians, Historians, Hunters and Collectors.* Harrisburg, Stackpole and Heck, 1947. 488 pp.

——. *Textbook of Firearms Investigation, Identification and Evidence.* Marines, Small Arms Technical Publishing Co., 1935. 875 pp.

U. S. Federal Bureau of Investigation. ★*Firearms Identification.* Washington, 33 pp.

E. *Moulage*

CLARKE, CARL D.: *Molding and Casting.* 2nd ed. Baltimore, Standard Arts Press, 1946. 300 pp.

NEBERGALL, R. W.: Moulage, *in* Rollin M. Perkins, *Elements of Police Science.* Chicago, Foundation Press, 1942. pp. 110–116.

F. *Personal Descriptions*

California. Department of Education. Bureau of Trade and Industrial Education. *Descriptions of Persons and Portrait Parle.*° Sacramento, 1949. 23 pp.

U. S. Federal Bureau of Investigation. ★*Personal Descriptions—Portrait Parle and Speaking Likeness.*

WENTWORTH, BERT, AND HARRIS HAWTHORNE WILDER. *Personal Identification: Methods for Identification of Individuals, Living and Dead.* Boston, Badger, 1918. 374 pp.

G. *Photography*

Eastman Kodak Company. ★*Photography in Law Enforcement.* Rochester, The Company, 1948. 112 pp.

RADLEY, J. A.: *Photography in Crime Detection.* London, Chapman and Hall, 1948. 186 pp.

SCOTT, CHARLES C.: *Photographic Evidence.* Kansas City, Vernon Law Book Co., 1942. 922 pp.

U. S. Navy Department. *Photography.* Washington, Government Printing Office, 1947. 2 vols.

H. *Questioned Document*

JONES, LLOYD L.: *Valid or Forged?* New York, Fund and Wagnalls, 1938. 168 pp.

LEE, CLARENCE DUNLAP, AND R. A. ABBEY: *Classification and Identification of Handwriting.* Toronto, Carswell, 1931. 113 pp.

MITCHELL, C. A.: *Documents and Their Scientific Examination.* London, Griffin, 1922. 215 pp.

OSBORN, ALBERT S.: *Problems of Proof.* 2nd ed. New York, The Author, 1926. 539 pp.

——. *Questioned Document Problems; the Discovery and Proof of the Facts.* Rev. ed. New York, Boyd, 1946. 569 pp.

——. *Questioned Documents.* 2nd ed. Albany, Boyd Printing Co., 1929. 1028 pp.

IX. COMMUNICATIONS

A. *General*

LEONARD, V. A.: *Police Communication Systems.* Berkeley, University of California Press, 1938. 589 pp.

X. JAIL—DETENTION—CUSTODIAL CARE

A. *Management*

U. S. Department of Justice. Bureau of Prisons. ★*Manual of Jail Management.* Washington, Government Printing Office, 1948. 38 pp.

B. *Practice and Procedure*

California. Department of Education. Bureau of Trade and Industrial Education. ★*Jail Practice and Procedure.*＊ Sacramento, 1949. 97 pp.

DeVINE, RUSSELL B.: *The American Jail.* New York, American Prison Association, 1937. 24 pp.

ROBINSON, LOUIS N.: *Jails, Care and Treatment of Misdemeanant Prisoners in the United States.* Philadelphia, Winston, 1944. 296 pp.

PIGEON, HELEN D., and others: *Principles and Methods in Dealing with Offenders.* State College, Pa., Pennsylvania Municipal Publications Service, 1948. 442 pp.

C. *Probation and Parole*

PIGEON, HELEN D.: *Probation and Parole in Theory and Practice; A Study Manual.* New York, National Probation Association, 1942. 420 pp.

D. *Standards*

California. State Board of Corrections. Committee on Jails. ★*Minimum Jail Standards.* Sacramento, 1946. 24 pp.

HART, HASTINGS H.: *Plans for City Police Jails and Village Lockups.* New York, Russell Sage Foundation, 1932. 27 pp.

U. S. Federal Security Agency. National Advisory Policy Committee on Social Protection. ★*Recommendations on Standards for Detention of Juveniles and Adults.* Washington, Government Printing Office, 1945. 24 pp.

CABOT, PHILIPPE, SIDNEY DE Q.: *Juvenile Delinquency: A Critical Annotated Bibliography.* New York, H. W. Wilson, 1946. 166 pp.

CULVER, DOROTHY C.: ★*Bibliography of Crime and Criminal Justice.* 1927–1931. New York, H. W. Wilson, 1934. 413 pp.

——. ★*Bibliography of Crime and Criminal Justice, 1932–1937.* New York, H. W. Wilson, 1939. 391 pp.

GRAZIA, ALFRED DE: *Human Relations in Public Administration.* Chicago, Public Administration Service, 1949. 52 pp.

GREER, SARAH: *A Bibliography of Police Administration and Police Science.* New York, Institute of Public Administration, 1936. 152 pp.

National Probation Association. *A Bookshelf for Probation and Parole Officers and Others Interested in Delinquency.* New York, 1947. 32 pp.

TOMPKINS, DOROTHY C., comp.: ★*The Crime Problem in California— A Selected Bibliography.* Berkeley. University of California, Bureau of Public Administration, 1947. 16 pp.

——. *Sabotage and Its Prevention.* War Bibliographies No. 1. Berkeley: University of California, Bureau of Public Administration, 1942. 24 pp.

——. *Sources for the Study of the Administration of Criminal Justice.* Sacramento, The California State Board of Corrections, Special Crime Study Commission, 1949. 294 pp.

U. S. Civil Service Commission. *Efficiency Ratings, 1940–45, A Selected List of References.* Washington: Government Printing Office, 1946.

Wagner, Allen H.: *Probation: A Selected Bibliography on the Individualized Treatment of the Offender.* Bibliography No. 2. New York, Russell Sage Foundation, 1948. 12 pp.

BIBLIOGRAPHY
Arranged Alphabetically

Abrahamsen, David: *Crime and the Human Mind.* New York, Columbia University Press, 1944. 244 pp.

Adams, Freeman H.: *★Basic Criminal Psychiatry with Emphasis on Sex Crimes.*° Sacramento, Department of Education, Peace Officers' Training, 1950.

Adlow, Elijah: *★Policemen and the Public.* Boston, Rochfort, 1947. 89 pp.

Allen, Edward L.: *American Jiu-Jitsu.* Toronto, Blue Ribbon, 1942.

American Academy of Political and Social Science. Gambling, *The Annals.* 269 (May, 1950). 1–149.

——. Juvenile Delinquency, *The Annals.* 261 (Jan., 1949).

American Red Cross. *First Aid Text-Book.* Rev. ed. Philadelphia, Blakiston, 1940. 256 pp.

American Society of Planning Officials. *A Manual of Recommended Personnel Standards in Public Planning.* Chicago, The Society, 1949. 37 pp.

Askins, Charles: *The Art of Handgun Shooting.* New York, Barnes, 1941. 219 pp.

Atcherly, Llewelyn W., and F. Brook: *Modus Operandi.* London, His Majesty's Stationery Office, 1932. 90 pp.

Aurner, Robert R.: *Effective Business English.* 3rd ed. Cincinnati, South-Western, 1949. 582 pp.

Baker, Russell: *Manual on the Law of Arrest, Search and Seizure.* Chicago, Chicago Crime Commission, 1944. 49 pp.

Barnes, Harry E., and Negley K. Teeters: *New Horizons in Criminology; the American Crime Problem.* New York, Prentice-Hall, 1946. 1069 pp.

Battley, Harry: *Single Fingerprints.* New Haven, Yale University Press, 1931. 98 pp.

Beckman, R. O.: *★How to Train Supervisors.* 3rd rev. ed. New York, Harper, 1948. 329 pp.

Bennett, Richard O.: *The Bicycle and Traffic Safety.* Evanston, Northwestern University Traffic Safety Institute, (1937). 75 pp.

Bingham, Walter Van Dyke, and Bruce Victor Moore: *How to Interview.* 3rd rev. ed. New York, Harper, 1941. 263 pp.

Black, Russell Van Nest: *Planning for the Small American City.* Rev. ed. Chicago, Public Administration Service, 1944. 86 pp.

Boos, William F. *The Poison Trail.* Boston, Cushman and Fling, 1939. 380 pp.

Brenham, Vernon C., and Samuel B. Kutash, eds.: *Encyclopedia of Criminology.* New York, Philosophical Library, 1949. 527 pp.

Bridges, B. C.: *Practical Fingerprinting.* New York, Funk and Wagnalls, 1942. 374 pp.

Broaded, C. H.: *★Essentials of Management for Supervisors.* New York, Harpers, 1947. 239 pp.

BROMBERG, WALTER: *Crime and the Mind; An Outline of Psychiatric Criminology.* Philadelphia, Lippincott, 1948. 219 pp.

BROOKS, PHILIP C.: *Public Records Management.* Chicago, Public Administration Service, 1949. 19 pp.

BUTLER, J. F.: Revolver Shooting, *in* Rollin M. Perkins, *Elements of Police Science.* Chicago, Foundation Press, 1942. pp 194–219.

CABOT, PHILIPPE, SIDNEY DE Q.: *Juvenile Delinquency; A Critical Annotated Bibliography.* New York, H. W. Wilson, 1946. 166 pp.

CAHALANE, CORNELIUS F.: *The Policeman.* New York, Dutton, 1923. 354 pp.

——. ★*Police Practices and Procedure.* New York, Dutton, 1914. 241 pp.

California. Department of Education. Bureau of Trade and Industrial Education. *Arson Investigation.*★ Sacramento, 1949. 16 pp.

——. *Basic Course in Firearms.*★ Sacramento, 1949. 25 pp.

——. *Bunco.*★ Sacramento, 1949. 12 pp.

——. *Burglary—Commercial.*★ Sacramento, 1949. 6 pp.

——. *Burglary—Residence.*★ Sacramento, 1949. 7 pp.

——. *Burglary—Safes.*★ Sacramento, 1949. 10 pp.

——. *Civil Process and Procedure.*★ Sacramento, 1949. 16 pp.

——. ★*Collection and Preservation of Evidence.*★ Sacramento, 1949. 22 pp.

——. *Conference Leader Training.* Sacramento, 1943. 39 pp.

——. *Corporate Security Frauds.*★ Sacramento, 1949. 6 pp.

——. *Court Appearance and Testimony.*★ Sacramento, 1949. 11 pp.

——. *Covering Roads for Wanted Cars and Fugitives.*★ Sacramento, 1949. 5 pp.

——. ★*Criminal Law Course, Student Officers' Work Outline Emphasizing Elements of Major Crime.*★ Sacramento, 1949. 109 pp.

——. ★*Criminal Law Outline.*★ Sacramento, 1949. 109 pp.

——. *Descriptions of Persons and Portrait Parle.*★ Sacramento, 1949. 23 pp.

——. ★*Drunk Driver Testing—Use of Chemical Tests for Intoxication.*★ Sacramento, 1949. 53 pp.

——. ★*Elements of Interrogation.*★ Sacramento, 1949. 79 pp.

——. ★*Elements of Police Investigation.*★ Sacramento, 1949. 13 pp.

——. *Extradition and and Rendition.*★ Sacramento, 1949. 13 pp.

——. ★*Field Note Taking.*★ Sacramento, 1950. 31 pp.

——. *Fingerprint Identification and Classification.*★ Sacramento, 1949. 13 pp.

——. *Grand Theft—Person.*★ Sacramento, 1949. 7 pp.

——. *Investigation of Auto Theft with Particular Reference to Modus Operandi.*★ Sacramento, 1949. 26 pp.

——. *Investigation of Fictitious Checks.*★ Sacramento, 1949. 6 pp.

——. *Investigation of Homicide.*★ Sacramento, 1949. 23 pp.

——. *Investigation of Prostitution.*★ Sacramento, 1949. 11 pp.

——. *Investigation of Sex Crimes.*★ Sacramento, 1949. 20 pp.

——. ★*Jail Practice and Procedure.*★ Sacramento, 1949. 97 pp.

——. *Juvenile Delinquency Control.*★ Sacramento, 1949. 33 pp.

——. *Juvenile Procedure.*★ Sacramento, 1949. 10 pp.

——. ★*Laboratory Techniques in Criminal Investigation.*★ Sacramento, 1949. 25 pp.

——. *Law of Arrest.*★ Sacramento, 1949. 21 pp.

——. ★*Modus Operandi Report Writing.*★ Sacramento, 1949. 22 pp.

——. *Narcotic Investigation and Narcotic Enforcement.*★ Sacramento, 1949. 19 pp.

——. ★*Patrol Procedure and Observation.** Sacramento, 1949. 20 pp.
——. ★*Police Organization and Administration.** Sacramento, 1950.
——. ★*Police Procedures.** Sacramento, 1949. 64 pp.
——. *Police Records.** Sacramento, 1949. 9 pp.
——. ★*Powers and Duties of the Sheriff and Other County Offices.** Sacramento, 1949. 13 pp.
——. *Public Relations.** Sacramento, 1949. 8 pp.
——. *Public Relations.** Sacramento, 1949. 11 pp.
——. *Public Speaking.** Sacramento, 1949. 8 pp.
——. ★*Report Writing.** Sacramento, 1949. 12 pp.
——. *Robbery.** Sacramento, 1949. 4 pp.
——. *Rules of Evidence.** Sacramento, 1949. 21 pp.
——. *Self-Defense.** Sacramento, 1949. 15 pp.
——. *Source of Information.** Sacramento, 1949. 29 pp.
——. ★*A Study Manual and Bibliography for Peace Officers.** Sacramento, 1950.
——. *Surveillance.** Sacramento, 1949. 35 pp.
——. ★*Traffic Accident Investigation.** Sacramento, 1949. 23 pp.
——. *Traffic Accident Records and Analysis.** Sacramento, 1949. 14 pp.
——. *Traffic Engineering (Outline).** Sacramento, 1949. 9 pp.
——. *Traffic (Selective) Enforcement.** Sacramento, 1949. 6 pp.
——. ★*Transportation of Prisoners.** Sacramento, 1949. 4 pp.
——. *Use of Records.** Sacramento, 1949. 28 pp.
California. Department of Justice. ★*A Guide to Race Relations for Peace Officers,* by Davis McEntire and Robert E. Powers. Sacramento, 1946. 38 pp.
——. ★*Peace Officers Manual on Juvenile Control.* Sacramento, 1944. 44 pp.
——. Division of Criminal Identification and Investigation. ★*Modus Operandi and Crime Reporting.* Sacramento, 1947. 17 pp.
——. Division of Narcotic Enforcement. *Narcotic Act.* Sacramento, 1949. 29 pp.
California. Governor. Coordinating Committee of State Officials on Traffic Safety. *Plan of Action for Traffic Safety in California.* Sacramento, 1949. 22 pp.
California. Highway Patrol. Division of Technical Services. *Auto Theft Investigation.* Sacramento, 1950. 36 pp.
California. Legislature. Interim Committee on Judicial System and Judicial Process. ★*Preliminary Report of the Subcommittee on Sex Crimes.* Sacramento, 1949. 269 pp.
California. State Board of Corrections. Committee on Jails. *Minimum Jail Standards.* Sacramento, 1946. 24 pp.
California. State Board of Equalization. ★*California Alcoholic Beverage Control Act and Related Constitutional Provisions.* Sacramento, 1949. 114 pp.
——. ★*Rules and Regulations Issued in Pursuance of Section 22 of Article XX of the Constitution of California and Alcoholic Beverage Control Act.* Sacramento, 1950. 24 pp.
California. Youth Authority. ★*California Laws Relating to Youthful Offenders, including the Youth Authority Act, the Juvenile Court Law.* Sacramento, 1947. 92 pp.
——. ★*The Youth Authority, Organization and Program.* Sacramento, 1945. 24 pp.
——. Division of Delinquency Prevention. ★*An Outline of a Community Program for the Prevention of Juvenile Delinquency.* Sacramento, 1943. 12 pp.

CALLAN, GEORGE D., AND RICHARD STEPHENSON: *Police Methods for Today and Tomorrow.* Newark, Duncan Press, 1939. 361 pp.

CASTELLANOS, I.: *Identification Problems, Criminal and Civil.* New York, Basuino, 1939. 215 pp.

CAVAN, RUTH S.: *Criminology.* New York, Crowell, 1948. 762 pp.

Chicago Crime Commission. *Police Standards.* Chicago, The Commission, 1942. 5 pp.

Chicago. Park District. *The Police and Minority Groups; A Manual Prepared for Use in the Chicago Park District Police Training School,* by Joseph D. Lohman. Chicago, 1947. 133 pp.

Civil Service Assembly. *Employee Relations in the Public Service.* Chicago, The Assembly, 1942. 246 pp.

——. *Employee Training in the Public Service.* Chicago, The Assembly, 1941. 172 pp.

——. *Oral Tests in Public Personnel Selection.* Chicago, The Assembly, 1943. 164 pp.

——. *Placement and Probation in the Public Service.* Chicago, The Assembly, 1946. 201 pp.

——. *Position-Classification in the Public Service.* Chicago, The Assembly, 1941. 404 pp.

——. *Recruiting Applicants for the Public Service.* Chicago, The Assembly, 1942. 200 pp.

CLARKE, CARL D.: *Molding and Casting.* 2nd ed. Baltimore, Standard Arts Press, 1946. 300 pp.

COOPER, ROBERT W.: *Municipal Police Administration in Texas.* Austin, University of Texas. 1938. 320 pp.

Council of State Governments. *The Handbook of Interstate Crime Control.* Rev. ed. Chicago, The Council, 1949. 91 pp.

——. *Highway Safety—Motor Truck Regulation.* Chicago, The Council, 1950. 198 pp.

CULVER, DOROTHY C.: ★*Bibliography of Crime and Criminal Justice, 1927–1931.* New York, H. W. Wilson, 1934. 413 pp.

——. ★*Bibliography of Crime and Criminal Justice, 1932–1937.* New York, H. W. Wilson, 1939. 391 pp.

CUSHMAN, FRANK, AND ROBERT W. CUSHMAN: *Improving Supervision.* New York, Wiley, 1947. 232 pp.

CUSHMAN, FRANK: ★*Training Procedure.* New York, Wiley, 1940. 230 pp.

DAVID, LEON T.: *The Tort Liability of Public Officers.* Chicago, Public Administration Service, 1940. 93 pp.

DAWSON, WILLIAM S.: ★*Aids to Psychiatry.* 5th ed. Baltimore, Williams and Wilkins, 1944. 306 pp.

DAY, CARL E.: *Handbook of California Evidence.* San Francisco, The Author, 1948. 192 pp.

Detroit. Bureau of Governmental Research. *Police Precincts; How Many Precincts are Necessary for Efficient and Economical Operations of the Police Department.* Report No. 159. Detroit, 1945. 17 pp.

DeVINE, RUSSELL B.: *The American Jail.* New York, American Prison Association, 1937. 24 pp.

DIENSTEIN, WILLIAM: *Technics For The Crime Investigator.* Charles C Thomas, Publisher, Springfield, Illinois, 1952. 222 pp.

DONIGAN, ROBERT L.: *Chemical Test Case Law*. Evanston, Northwestern University Traffic Institute, 1950. 83 pp.

Eastman Kodak Company. ★*How to Make Good Pictures*. 28th ed. Rochester, The Company, 1949. 240 pp.

——. ★*Photography in Law Enforcement*. Rochester, The Company, 1948. 112 pp.

EISEMAN, JAMES S.: *Elements of Investigative Techniques*. Bloomington, McKnight and McKnight, 1949. 182 pp.

ELLINGSTON, JOHN R.: *Protecting Our Children from Criminal Careers*. New York, Prentice-Hall, 1948. 374 pp.

EVANS, HENRY K., AND F. M. KREML: ★*Traffic Engineering and the Police*. Rev. ed. Evanston, International Association of Chiefs of Police and National Conservation Bureau, 1946. 103 pp.

FISHER, EDWARD: ★*People's Court*. Evanston, Northwestern University Traffic Institute, 1947. 164 pp.

FISHER, JACOB: *The Art of Detection*. New Brunswick, Rutgers University Press, 1947. 248 pp.

FORRESTER, GLENN C.: *The Use of Chemical Tests for Alcohol in Traffic Law Enforcement*. Springfield, Illinois, Charles C Thomas, Publisher, 1949. 250 pp.

FRICKE, CHARLES W.: ★*California Criminal Evidence*. Los Angeles, O. W. Smith, 1945. 404 pp.

——. ★*California Criminal Law*. 3rd ed. Los Angeles, O. W. Smith, 1949. 470 pp.

——. ★*California Criminal Procedure*. 2nd rev. ed. Los Angeles, O. W. Smith, 1949. 470 pp.

——. ★*California Peace Officers' Manual*. Rev. 7th ed. Los Angeles, O. W. Smith, 1949. 259 pp.

——. ★*Criminal Investigation*. Popular ed. Los Angeles, O. W. Smith, 1949. 79 pp.

——. *Digest of California Criminal Decisions, 1942–1947*. Los Angeles, Peace Officers Civil Service Ass'n., 1947. 205 pp.

——. *5000 Criminal Definitions, Terms and Phrases*. 2nd ed. Los Angeles, O. W. Smith, 1949. 121 pp.

——. *1000 Police Questions and Answers for the California Peace Officer*. 4th ed. Los Angeles, O. W. Smith, 1946. 75 pp.

GESELL, HAROLD J. E.: Fingerprints, *in* Rollin M. Perkins, *Elements of Police Science*. Chicago, Foundation Press, 1942. pp. 144–180.

GOCKE, B. W.: ★*Police Sergeants Manual*. Los Angeles, O. W. Smith, 1946. 312 pp.

GRAVES, WILLIAM B.: ★*Public Administration in a Democratic Society*. Boston: Heath, 1950. 759 pp.

GRAZIA, ALFRED DE: *Human Relations in Public Administration*. Chicago, Public Administration Service, 1949. 52 pp.

GREER, SARAH: *A Bibliography of Police Administration and Police Science*. New York, Institute of Public Administration, 1936. 152 pp.

GROSS, HANS:. ★*Criminal Investigation*. London, Sweet and Maxwell, 1938. 586 pp.

GULICK, LUTHER, AND L. URWICK: ★*Papers on the Science of Administration*. New York, Columbia University, Institute of Public Administration, 1937. 195 pp.

HALSEY, MAXWELL N.: *Traffic Accidents and Congestion.* New York, Wiley, 1947. 408 pp.

HALSEY, GEORGE D.: *Supervising People.* New York, Harper, 1946. 233 pp.

HAMMOND, HAROLD F.: ★*Traffic Engineering Handbook.* New York, Institute of Traffic Engineers, National Conservation Bureau, 1941. 320 pp.

HAMMOND, H. F., AND F. M. KREML: *Traffic Engineering and the Police.* Evanston, Northwestern Traffic Institute, 1938. 285 pp.

HART, HASTINGS, H.: *Plans for City Police Jails and Village Lockups.* New York, Russell Sage Foundation, 1932. 27 pp.

HATCHER, JULIAN S.: *Notebook; a Standard Reference Book for Shooters, Gunsmiths, Ballisticians, Historians, Hunters and Collectors.* Harrisburg, Stackpole and Heck, 1947. 488 pp.

——. *Textbook of Firearms Investigation, Identification, and Evidence.* Marines, Small Arms Technical Publishing Co., 1935. 875 pp.

HENTIG, HANS VON: *Crime; Causes and Condition.* New York, McGraw-Hill, 1947. 379 pp.

HERZOG, A. S., AND A. J. EZICKSON: *Camera Take the Stand.* New York, Prentice-Hall, 1940. 195 pp.

HESSE, ERICH: *Narcotics and Drug Addiction.* Tr. by Frank Gaynor. New York, Philosophical Library, 1946. 219 pp.

HOLCOMB, RICHARD L.: *The Police and the Public.* Iowa City, State University of Iowa, Institute of Public Affairs, 1950. 36 pp.

——. *Police Patrol.* Charles C Thomas, Publisher, Springfield, Illinois, 1952. 115 pp.

——. ★*Selection of Police Officers.* Iowa, State University of Iowa, Institute of Public Affairs, 1946. 94 pp.

HOLDEN, PAUL E., LOUNSBURY S. FISH, AND HUBERT L. SMITH: ★*Top-Management Organization and Control.* Stanford, University of Stanford Press, 1941. 239 pp.

HUBBARD, HENRY F.: *The Elements of a Comprehensive Personnel Program.* Chicago, Civil Service Assembly, 1947. 17 pp.

HUNT, J. McVICKER, ed.: *Personality and the Behavior Disorders.* New York, Ronald Press, 1944. 2 vols.

HUTZEL, ELEANOR L.: *Policewoman's Handbook.* New York, Columbia University Press, 1933. 303 pp.

INBAU, FRED E.: ★*Lie Detection and Criminal Interrogation.* 2nd rev. ed. Baltimore, Williams and Wilkins, 1948. 193 pp.

Institute for Training in Municipal Administration. ★*Municipal Police Administration.* Rev. ed. Chicago, International City Managers' Association, 1950.

International Association of Chiefs of Police. ★*Police Unions and Other Police Organizations.* Washington, The Association, 1944. 30 pp.

——. ★*State Traffic Law Enforcement.* Chicago, The Association, 1944. 300 pp.

——. Committee on Uniform Crime Records. ★*Uniform Crime Reporting.* A *Complete Manual for Police.* Rev. ed. New York, The Association, 1929. 464 pp.

International City Managers' Association. *Monthly Administrative Reports for Cities.* Chicago, The Association, 1949. 32 pp.

——. ★*Municipal Personnel Administration.* Chicago, The Association, 1947. 435 pp.

——. *Municipal Public Relations.* Chicago, The Association, 1940. 50 pp.

——. *Specifications for the Annual Municipal Report.* Chicago, The Association, 1948. 52 pp.

——. *The Technique of Municipal Administration.* Chicago, The Association, 1947. 601 pp.

JACKEY, DAVID F., AND MELVIN L. BARLOW: ★*The Craftsman Prepares to Teach.* New York, Macmillan, 1944. 184 pp.

JARVIS, FRED J.: First Aid, *in* Rollin M. Perkins, *Elements of Police Science.* Chicago, Foundation Press, 1942. pp. 181–193.

JONES, LLOYD L.: *Valid or Forged?* New York, Funk and Wagnalls, 1938. 168 pp.

KENT, FREDERICK W.: Photography, *in* Rollin M. Perkins, *Elements of Police Science.* Chicago, Foundation Press, 1942. pp. 117–143.

KINSEY, A. C., W. B. POMEROY, AND C. E. MARTIN: ★*Sexual Behavior in the Human Male.* New York, Saunders, 1948. 804 pp.

KRAFFT-EBING, RICHARD VON: ★*Psychopathia Sexualis.* London, Rebman, 1901. 585 pp.

KREML, FRANK M.: ★*Evidence Handbook for Police.* Evanston, Northwestern University Traffic Institute, 1948. 150 pp.

KUWASHIMA, T. S.: *Judo; Forty-One Lessons in the Modern Science of Jiu-Jitsu.* New York, Putnam, 1949. 156 pp.

LADD, MASON: ★On the Witness Stand, *in* Rollin M. Perkins, *Elements of Police Science.* Chicago, Foundation Press, 1942. pp. 91–109.

LAIRD, DONALD A.: *The Technique of Handling People.* New York, McGraw-Hill, 1947. 138 pp.

——. *The Technique of Personal Analysis.* New York, McGraw-Hill, 1945. 408 pp.

LARSON, JOHN: *Lying and Its Detection.* Chicago, University of Chicago Press, 1932. 453 pp.

LEE, ALFRED McCLUNG, AND NORMAN DAYMOND HUMPHREY: *Race Riot.* New York, Dryden Press, 1943. 143 pp.

LEE, CLARENCE DUNLAP, AND R. A. ABBEY: *Classification and Identification of Handwriting.* Toronto, Carswell, 1931. 113 pp.

LEONARD, V. A.: *Police Communication Systems.* Berkeley, University of California Press, 1938. 589 pp.

——. *Police Organization and Management.* The Foundation Press. Brooklyn, 1951. 507 pp.

LEVIN, FRANK K.: ★*How to Read for Self-Improvement.* Chicago, American Technical Society, 1947. 246 pp.

LEWIS, ELMER A., comp.: *Crime, Kidnapping and Prison Laws.* Washington, Government Printing Office, 1941. 199 pp.

LINDESMITH, ALFRED: *Opiate Addiction.* Bloomington, Principia Press, 1947. 238 pp.

LINDNER, ROBERT M.: ★*Stone Walls and Men.* New York, Odyssey Press, 1946. 496 pp.

LUCAS, ALFRED: *Forensic Chemistry and Scientific Crime Investigation.* 4th ed. New York, Longmans, 1946. 340 pp.

MACCORKLE, STUART A.: *Municipal Administration.* New York, Prentice-Hall, 1942. 406 pp.

McDONALD, HUGH C., AND HARRY W. ROGERS: *The Classification of Police Photographs.* Los Angeles, De Vorss, 1941. 89 pp.

McDonald, John C.: ★*Crime is a Business.* Stanford, Stanford University Press, 1939. 363 pp.

Magnusson, Leifur: *Government and Union-Employer Relations: An Analysis of Statutes and Administrative Regulations.* Chicago, Public Administration Service, 1945. 36 pp.

Mason, Paul, comp.: ★*Constitution of the State of California and of the United States and Other Documents.* Sacramento, State Printing Office, 1949. 329 pp.

Matsuyama, Frank: *Yawara Manual.* Denver, The Author, 1948. 78 pp.

Merrill, Maud: *Problems of Child Delinquency.* New York, Houghton-Mifflin, 1947. 403 pp.

Michael, Jerome, and Herbert Wechsler: *Criminal Law and Its Administration.* Chicago, Foundation Press, 1940. 1410 pp.

Miles, Arnold: *How Criminals are Caught.* New York, Macmillan, 1939. 123 pp.

Mitchell, C. A.: *Documents and Their Scientific Examination.* London, Griffin, 1922. 215 pp.

Monroe, David G.: *State and Provincial Police; A Study in Police Functioning in the United States and Canada.* Chicago, International Association of Chiefs of Police, 1941. 251 pp.

Mosher, William E., and J. Donald Kingsley: ★*Public Personnel Administration.* New York, Harper, 1942. 671 pp.

Municipal Finance Officers Association. *Accounting for Governmental Supplies.* Chicago, The Association, 1940. 60 pp.

——. *Accounting for Government-Owned Motor Equipment.* Chicago, The Association, 1940. 60 pp.

——. *Municipal Budget Procedure and Budgetary Accounting.* Chicago, The Association, 1942. 100 pp.

Municipal Finance Officers Association. Committee on Public Employee Retirement Administration. *Retirement Plans for Public Employees.* Chicago, The Association, 1946. 36 pp.

National Probation Association. *A Bookshelf for Probation and Parole Officers and Others Interested in Delinquency.* New York, 1947. 32 pp.

Nebergall, R. W.: ★*Moulage,* in Rollin M. Perkins, *Elements of Police Science.* Chicago, Foundation Press, 1942. pp. 110–116.

Newton, Roy: *How to Improve Your Personality.* New York, McGraw-Hill, 1949. 205 pp.

Northwestern University Traffic Institute. ★*Accident Investigation Manual.* Rev. ed. Evanston, The Institute, 1948. 241 pp.

Odell, Margaret K., and Earl P. Strong: *Records Management and Filing Operations.* New York, McGraw-Hill, 1947. 342 pp.

O'Hara, Charles E. and James W. Osterburg: ★*An Introduction to Criminalistics.* New York, Macmillan, 1949. 705 pp.

Olander, Oscar G.: Police Courtesy, in Rollin M. Perkins, *Elements of Police Science.* Chicago, Foundation Press, 1942. pp. 73–90.

Osborn, Albert S.: Problems of Proof. 2nd ed. New York, The Author, 1926. 539 pp.

——. *Questioned Document Problems; the Discovery and Proof of the Facts.* Rev. ed. New York, Boyd, 1946. 569 pp.

——. *Questioned Documents.* 2nd ed. Albany, Boyd Printing Co., 1929. 1028 pp.

OWSLEY, ROY H.: *City Plans for Promoting Industrial Peace.* Chicago, American Municipal Association, 1947. 32 pp.

Peace Officers' Association of the State of California. *The Crime Prevention Committee's Report on Subversive Activities.* (1940). 19 pp.

PEPER, JOHN P., VOLLMER, AUGUST AND BOOLSEN, FRANK M.: *Police Organization and Administration.* California State Department of Education, Bureau of Industrial Education, Sacramento, 1951. 217 pp.

PERKINS, ROLLIN M.: ★*Elements of Police Science.* Chicago, Foundation Press, 1942. 615 pp.

——. ★*Police Examinations.* Brooklyn, Foundation Press, 1947. 431 pp.

PFIFFNER, JOHN: ★*A Manual for Administrative Analysts.* Los Angeles: University of Southern California, 1947.

——. ★*Public Administration.* Rev. ed. New York, Ronald Press, 1946. 621 pp.

——. ★*Supervision of Personnel.* Los Angeles, University of Southern California, 1949.

PIGEON, HELEN D., and others: *Principles and Methods in Dealing with Offenders.* State College, Pa., Pennsylvania Municipal Publications Service, 1948. 442 pp.

PIGEON, HELEN D.: *Probation and Parole In Theory and Practice; A Study Manual.* New York, National Probation Association, 1942. 420 pp.

PIGORS, PAUL, AND CHARLES A. MEYERS: ★*Personnel Administration.* New York, McGraw-Hill, 1947. 553 pp.

POLLAK, OTTO: *Criminality of Women.* Philadelphia, University of Pennsylvania Press, 1950. 180 pp.

PROBST, JOHN B.: *Measuring and Rating Employee Value.* New York, Ronald Press, 1947. 166 pp.

Public Administration Service. *Merit System Installation.* Chicago, Public Administration Service, 1941. 58 pp.

——. *Work Simplification: As Exemplified by the Work Simplification Program of the U. S. Bureau of the Budget.* Chicago, Public Administration Service, 1945. 49 pp.

PUTTKAMMER, ERNST W.: *Manual on Criminal Law Procedure.* Chicago, Chicago Crime Commission, 1946. 89 pp.

RADLEY, J. A.: *Photography in Crime Detection.* London, Chapman and Hall, 1948. 186 pp.

RECKLESS, WALTER C.: *The Crime Problem.* New York, Appleton-Century-Crofts, 1950. 537 pp.

RIVER, PAUL J.DE: *The Sexual Criminal.* Springfield, Illinois, Charles C Thomas, Publisher, 1949. 250, pp.

ROBINSON, LOUIS N.: *Jails, Care and Treatment of Misdemeanant Prisoners in the United States.* Philadelphia, Winston, 1944. 296 pp.

ROBINTON, WALTER H.: *Basic Procedure in Law Enforcement.* Gainesville, University of Florida, 1943. 140 pp.

ROETHLISBERGER, FRITZ J.: ★*Management and Morale.* Cambridge, Harvard University Press, 1941. 194 pp.

——. WILLIAM J. DICKSON, AND HAROLD A. WRIGHT: *Management and the Worker.* Cambridge, Harvard University Press, 1939. 615 pp.

ROPER, WALTER: *Pistol and Revolver Shooting.* New York, Macmillan, 1945. 256 pp.

SCHELL, ERWIN H.: *The Technique of Executive Control.* 6th ed. New York, McGraw-Hill, 1946. 270 pp.

SCOTT, CHARLES C.: *Photographic Evidence.* Kansas City, Vernon Law Book Co., 1942. 922 pp.

SCOTT, WALTER DILL, ROBERT C. CLOTHIER, AND WILLIAM R. SPRIEGEL: ★*Personnel Management.* 4th ed. New York, McGraw-Hill, 1949. 648 pp.

SIO, ARNOLD A.: *Parking—What Cities are Doing.* Chicago, American Municipal Association, 1949. 17 pp.

SKEHAN, JAMES J.: ★*Modern Police Work Including Detective Duty.* Rev. ed. New York, Basuino, 1948. 657 pp.

SMITH, BRUCE: *Police Systems in the United States.* Rev. ed. New York, Harper, 1949. 351 pp.

——. *Rural Crime Control.* New York, Institute of Public Administration, 1933. 306 pp.

——. *State Police.* New York, Macmillan, 1925. 281 pp.

SNYDER, LeMOYNE: ★*Homicide Investigation.* Springfield, Illinois, Charles C Thomas, Publisher, 1949. 302 pp.

SODERMAN, HARRY, AND JOHN J. O'CONNELL: *Modern Criminal Investigation.* Rev. ed. New York, Funk and Wagnalls, 1945. 478 pp.

Southern California. University. Delinquency Control Institute. ★*Administrative Aspects of Delinquency Control.* Los Angeles, University of Southern California, 1946. 74 pp.

——. ★*Delinquency Prevention Techniques.* Los Angeles, University of Southern California, 1947. 93 pp.

——. ★*Social Treatment Aspects of Delinquency Control.* Los Angeles, University of Southern California, 1946. 80 pp.

SPRIEGEL, WILLIAM R., AND EDWARD SCHULZ: ★*Elements of Supervision.* New York, Wiley, 1942. 273 pp.

STONE, DONALD C.: ★*Recruitment of Policemen.* Chicago, International Association of Chiefs of Police, 1938. 28 pp.

SULLIVAN, J. J.: *Criminal Procedure in Municipal, Justice, and City Courts of California.* St. Paul, West, 1948. 498 pp.

SUTHERLAND, EDWIN H.: *Principles of Criminology.* 4th ed. Chicago, Lippincott, 1947. 634 pp.

TAFT, DONALD R.: *Criminology.* New York, Macmillan, 1942. 708 pp.

TAYLOR, CLARENCE P.: ★*A Traffic Officer's Training Manual.* Chicago, National Safety Council, 1930. 225 pp.

TEAD, ORDWAY: *Art of Leadership.* New York, McGraw-Hill, 1935. 308 pp.

THORPE, LOUIS P., AND BARNEY KATZ: *The Psychology of Abnormal Behavior.* New York, Ronald Press, 1948. 877 pp.

TOMPKINS, DOROTHY CAMPBELL: *Sabotage and Its Prevention.* War Bibliographies No. 1. Berkeley, University of California, Bureau of Public Administration, 1942. 24 pp.

TOMPKINS, DOROTHY C., comp.: ★*The Crime Problem in California—A Selected Bibliography.* Berkeley, University of California, Bureau of Public Administration, 1947. 16 pp.

——. *Sources for the Study of the Administration of Criminal Justice.* Sacramento, The California State Board of Corrections, Special Crime Study Commission, 1949. 294 pp.

TRISKA, JOSEPH F.: ★*Juvenile Laws in California.* 2nd ed. Los Angeles, 1948. 380 pp.

TURNER, RALPH F.: ★*Forensic Science and Laboratory Techniques.* Springfield, Illinois, Charles C Thomas, Publisher, 1949. 242 pp.

U. S. Civil Service Commission. *Efficiency Ratings, 1940–45, A Selected List of References.* Washington, Government Printing Office, 1946.

——. ★*Firearms Identification.* Washington, 33 pp.

——. ★*A Handbook Containing Suggestions for the Preparation of Uniform Crime Reports.* Washington, 1938. 31 pp.

——. ★*How to Use the Uniform Crime Reports.* Washington, 1939. 28 pp.

——. ★*Personal Descriptions—Portrait Parle and Speaking Likeness.* Washington, 23 pp.

U. S. Federal Bureau of Investigation. ★*Some Technical Observations in the Detection of Sabotage.* Washington, 1942. 44 pp.

——. *Traffic Control and Accident Investigation.* Chapel Hill, University of North Carolina, Institute of Government, 1947. 197 pp.

——. ★*Uniform Crime Reporting Handbook; Suggestions on Uniform Crime Reports.* Washington, 1943. 33 pp.

U. S. Federal Security Agency. *Techniques of Law Enforcement Against Prostitution.* Washington, Government Printing Office, 1943. 75 pp.

U. S. Federal Security Agency. Children's Bureau. ★*Techniques of Law Enforcement in the Treatment of Juveniles and the Prevention of Juvenile Delinquency.* Washington, Government Printing Office, 1944. 60 pp.

——. ★*Understanding Juvenile Delinquency.* Washington, Government Printing Office, 1943. 52 pp.

U. S. National Security Agency. National Advisory Policy Committee on Social Protection. ★*Recommendations on Standards for Detention of Juveniles and Adults.* Washington, Government Printing Office, 1945. 24 pp.

U. S. Navy Department. *Photography.* Washington: Government Printing Office, 1947. 2 vols.

U. S. War Department. ★*Criminal Investigation.* Field Manual FM 19–20. Washington, Government Printing Office, 1946. 358 pp.

VOLLMER, AUGUST: ★*The Criminal.* Brooklyn, Foundation Press, 1949. 462 pp.

——. Criminal Investigation, *in* Rollin M. Perkins, *Elements of Police Science.* Chicago, Foundation Press, 1942. pp. 37–59.

——. *The Police and Modern Society.* Berkeley, University of California Press, 1936. 253 pp.

——. AND ALFRED E. PARKER: *Crime and the State Police.* Berkeley, University of California Press, 1935. 226 pp.

WAGNER, ALLAN H.: *Probation; A Selected Bibliography on the Individualized Treatment of the Offender.* Bibliography No. 2. New York, Russell Sage Foundation, 1948. 12 pp.

WAITE, JOHN B.: *Criminal Law and Its Enforcement.* 3rd ed. Brooklyn, Foundation Press, 1947. 902 pp.

WALTON, ROBERT P. *Marihuana, America's New Drug Problem.* Philadelphia: Lippincott, 1938. 223 pp.

WARREN, GEORGE: ★*Traffic Court.* New York, Little, Brown, 1942. 280 pp.

WELLMAN, F. L.: *The Art of Cross-Examination.* 4th ed. rev. New York, Macmillan, 1944. 479 pp.

WENTWORTH, BERT, AND HARRIS HAWTHORNE WILDER. *Personal Identification: Methods for Identification of Individuals, Living and Dead.* Boston, Badger, 1918. 374 pp.

WERTHAM, FREDERIC: *Show of Violence.* New York, Doubleday, 1949. 279 pp.

WHITE, LEONARD D.: *★Introduction to the Study of Public Administration.* 3rd ed. New York, Macmillan, 1948. 612 pp.

WIGMORE, JOHN H.: *★Code of the Rules of Evidence in Trials at Law.* 3rd ed. Boston, Little, Brown, 1942. 620 pp.

——. *Science of Judicial Proof.* 3rd ed. rev. Boston, Little, Brown, 1937. 1065 pp.

WILLIAMS, CAROL M.: *Organization and Practices of Policewomen Divisions in the United States.* Detroit, National Training School of Public Service, 1946. 40 pp.

WILSON, FRANK J.: *Detection of Counterfeit Money, in* Rollin M. Perkins, *Elements of Police Science.* Chicago, Foundation Press, 1942. pp. 61–72.

WILSON, O. W.: *Distribution of Police Patrol.* Chicago, Public Administration Service, 1941. 27 pp.

——. *Police Administration.* New York, McGraw-Hill Book Co., 1950. 540 pp.

——. *Police Planning.* Springfield, Illinois: Charles C Thomas, Publisher, 1952. 500 pp.

——. *★Police Records: Their Installation and Use.* 2nd ed. Chicago, Public Administration Service, 1948. 336 pp.

WOOD, STERLING A.: *Riot Control.* Harrisburg, Military Service Publishing Co., 1946. 155 pp.

THIS BOOK

A RECRUIT
ASKS SOME QUESTIONS

By JOHN P. PEPER

was set and printed by The Mack Printing Company of Easton, Pennsylvania and bound by Arnold's Book Bindery of Reading, Pennsylvania. The page trim size is 6 × 9 inches. The type page is 26 × 43 picas. The type face is Linotype Caledonia, set 11 point on 13 point. The text paper is 60-pound Westvaco Eggshell. The cover is Holliston Sturdite 7X-73206-L5 Morocco, Two-tone Red.

With THOMAS BOOKS *careful attention is given to all details of manufacturing and design. It is the Publisher's desire to present books that are satisfactory as to their physical qualities and artistic possibilities and appropriate for their particular use.* THOMAS BOOKS *will be true to those laws of quality that assure a good name and good will.*